# *MANTLE OF THE SKIES*

Mount Sefton at sunrise

Memorial to Sydney King, Darby Thomson and John Richmond, first men to die on Mount Cook (seen in background) in 1914. At entrance to Hooker Valley

# MANTLE OF THE SKIES

*THE SOUTHERN ALPS OF NEW ZEALAND*

by Philip Temple

WHITCOMBE & TOMBS

# Contents



# Illustrations

All photographs were taken by the author, with the exception of the four detailed below. Information about camera equipment and film can be found on the last page of this book.
John Johns of the New Zealand Forest Service kindly supplied the photographs of red deer and chamois on page 31, also the colour transparency of the Mount Cook lily on page 107. The transparency of the ice climber on page 117 is a photograph of the author taken by a climbing companion.
The bird motif photographs are all of the kea (*Nestor notabilis*), a parrot found only in the mountainous regions of the South Island of New Zealand.

Maps by J. K. Macdonald.

*Jacket photograph*: Sunset on Mount Tasman.



*Opposite* Cloud and mist parting after heavy rain in the Copland Valley

## Acknowledgments

The author wishes to thank Mr and Mrs J. Aspinall, Mr D. Burnett and Mrs R. St Barbe Baker for help and hospitality; Dave White and David Galloway for companionship above the snowline; Mount Cook Air Services for assistance with aerial photographs; Bill Beavis for advice and work with black and white films; Noel Hilliard and Ray Knox for criticism of the manuscript; my wife Daphne for typing the manuscript and for invaluable comment and encouragement.

Grateful acknowledgment is made to the following for the use of copyright quotations: The Caxton Press, Christchurch, and the estate of Mary Ursula Bethell for the extract from 'By Burkes Pass' (page 11); the Caxton Press and Mr James K. Baxter for the extracts from 'Poem in the Matukituki Valley' and 'The Mountains' (pages 65 and 113); the Pegasus Press, Christchurch, and Mr Denis Glover for the extract from 'Arawata Bill' (page 89).

ISBN 0 7233 0301 0 W&T G5322



*Published by Whitcombe & Tombs Ltd, Christchurch*

*Designed by Philip Temple and the publisher's editorial staff. Composition (in 13 on 14 point Perpetua with Univers for display) by Whitcombe & Tombs*

*Colour separations and printing and binding in Japan under the supervision of John Weatherhill Inc., Tokyo*

# INTRODUCTION

'THE SOUTHERN ALPS'—a simple name for an alien range, given by British voyagers seeking to understand and possess with the sound of familiar words. A high land, a barren white presence in the sky, compelling admiration . . . .

'KAHURANGI—MANTLE OF THE SKIES'—a strong-flowing Maori name that speaks of cloud and snow shrouding the cliffs and towers of range upon range; mountains of myths and gods, their flanks seamed with greenstone, *te pounamu*, and clothed by the abundant forest of a many-faced landscape . . . .

These mountains span the South Island of New Zealand from Nelson to Fiordland, for over three hundred miles, though a keen eye might detect the first uplifting of rock at the beaches of Cloudy Bay and not see it fall again until the colder shores of Foveaux Strait. The Southern Alps *are* the South Island: the ridges reach out to the sea on the north, west and south; the eastern foothills are precursors of greater heights and the eastern plains are created from mountain dross. No matter where one moves or lives in the island there is a presence of mountains.

Clearly, within the compass of one book, it is impossible to contain every facet, every fold and turn of such a vast and complicated landscape; to do that one would need a hundred scholars and a hundred books. But, by taking different parts of the whole and probing these with camera and pen, enlarging from personal experience and journeying, one can grasp the essential nature of the Southern Alps, appreciate the variety of landscape and picture the people who live or travel in it.

In this book we go to the heart of the Southern Alps, the big country of the Mackenzie and Mount Cook—tussock and ice, sheep stations and glaciers; then north to Arthur's Pass—the gentler scope of a mountain playground, threaded with history; south to the Mount Aspiring country of Otago—high winter ridges and a dictating river; over the Divide to Westland, where icefall and cataract course through the bush and the rain. Lastly, we move above the snowline, exploring the world of the mountaineer, his realm of frost and sun.

In picturing flowers and glaciers, writing of peaks and people, I offer views of mountains loved and respected, sometimes deeply comprehended, sometimes only glimpsed; a colourful impression to evoke the beauty, character and human relationship in a great range—Kahurangi, Mantle of the Skies.

PHILIP TEMPLE

# TUSSOCK AND ICE

## *Mount Cook and the Mackenzie Country*

Nature, earth's angel, man's antagonist,
    The stern antagonist from whom he wrests his bread,
Long heretofore with vast magnificence
    Did carve this scene, prepare the arena, spread
Bronze tussocked terraces before precipitous
    Great purple alps, loose glacier-shed
    Fierce-laughing streams in circuitous riverbed.

FROM 'By Burkes Pass'
BY Mary Ursula Bethell



*Opposite* Mount Cook (and Tasman) from Guide Hill

*Overleaf* The edge of the Hochstetter Icefall beneath the eastern face of Mount Cook

Mackenzie Pass

# *Tussock and Ice*

DRIVING SOUTH from Christchurch, leaving the crowd of suburban lights behind, picking up speed, was like a release. The ties of everyday life were cut and I felt a surge of excitement as if this was a unique adventure that only the three of us could share. Settling back, avoiding the glare of oncoming lights on the long straight highway, I tried consciously to rest before my turn at the wheel. It would be a tiring night, dulling the edge of anticipation; two hundred miles stretched into the darkness, and hard on the heels of excitement came sudden fatigue.

The tension of rushing to leave on time had now gone, replaced by weariness and pin-pricking doubts. Would the weather hold? If it rained the climb would be off, but then my conscience would be clear for sleeping the time away. If it was fine, would I be strong enough to keep up, did I have the courage to meet all manner of imagined disasters? Success was difficult to achieve and the mountains were unsympathetic and unforgiving. But then the purpose of the journey lay in 'giving it a go', not so much in the final achievement.

We left the main road and twisted through paddocks on lanes that ran through open country then lost themselves in tunnels of macrocarpa trees, that squeezed over one-way bridges and branched at confusing signposts. Traffic was thin now. Geraldine had already gone, still bright and untidy with the dregs of late-night shopping. We drove on in a fug of warmth and cigarette smoke, the vehicle and the moonless dark insulating us from the rich, rolling downs that curled on to the frosty hollow of Fairlie.

We stopped. A single milk bar sold pies, cigarettes and milk shakes and there were a few cars at the kerb outside like moths at the only light in town. I felt reassured about the climb as I walked round to the driver's seat. The sky glittered with stars and only a faint breeze from the east turned in the air.

The threads of human order dwindled as we drove towards the constricting hills that channelled us into Burkes Pass—narrow brown valleys that would heighten the climax of emerging on to the big Mackenzie Country beyond. Below the pass a light still burned in the hotel that was a staging point, a last chance for rest, before traversing the cold uplands beneath the main ranges. I remembered warm middays when I had stopped on the circle of green beneath the shading oak tree, drinking the traveller's earned beer, watching a peacock strut incongruously in its pen or the hills moving at Easter with dogs and sheep at the trials.

But now the hills were still, shrouded with thick mist in comforting scarves. We rushed at the long climb to the crest of the pass, where the headlights illumined serried pine trees, unreal in the mist, and the sudden sharp outline of the monument that exhorted 'Plant forest trees for your lives'. Trees to break the low line of tough tussock, to shelter the homesteads, comfort the stock, to soften the hostile horizon.

Tentatively, as the lights reflected off the fog, we picked up speed again, running into unknown country, tyres drumming on the hard chip of the road. My tired eyes searched



Hooker River

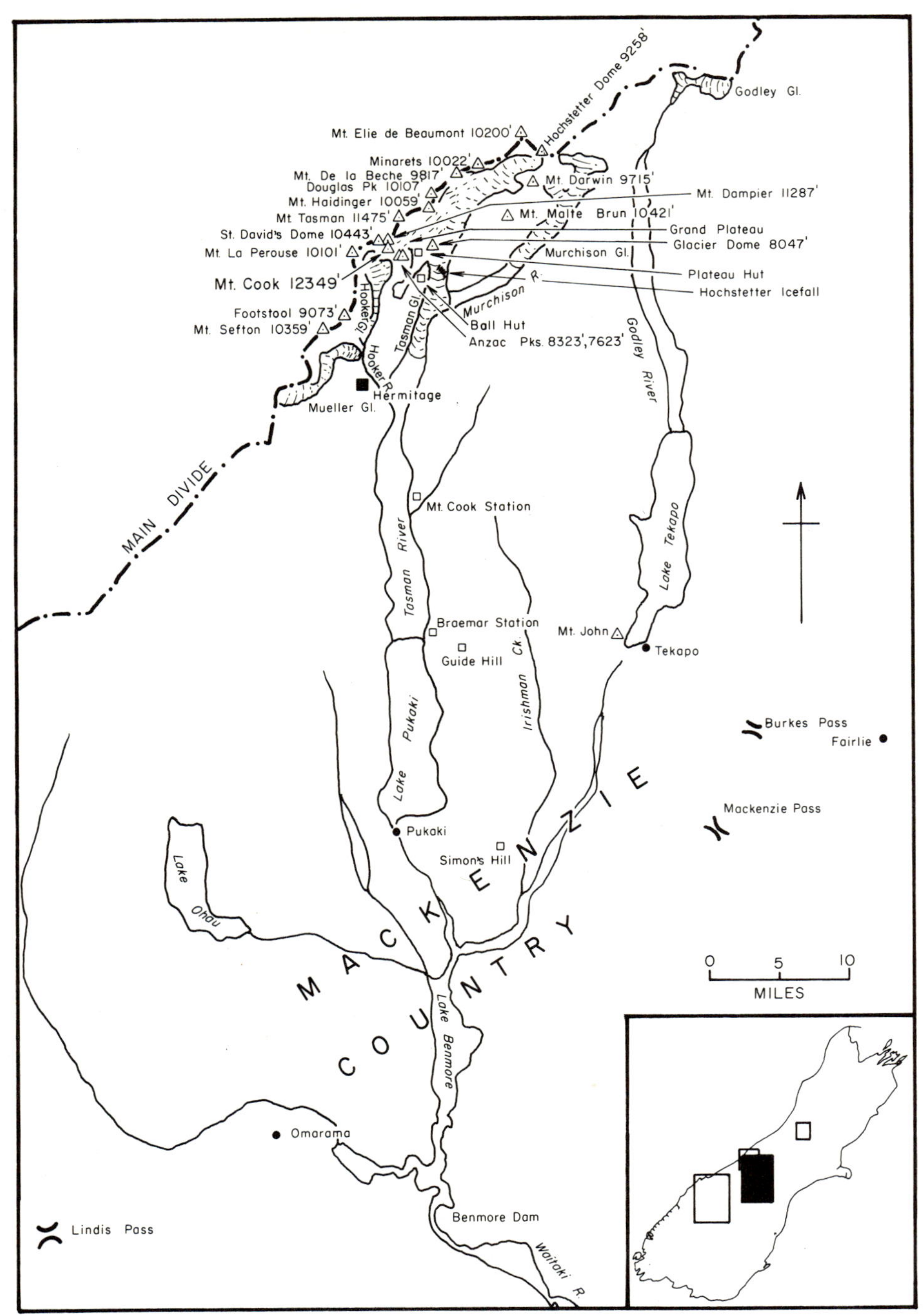


for a break in the fog, seeking a landscape that was dear to my heart; suddenly it seemed foolish that I should ever have elected to live away from it. Quickly, with a swirl, the fog broke, closed again, then parted cleanly to show the dark, hard hills of rock and grass. That moment was like moving into another dimension, a plane of nature unsuspected after the rich sheep paddocks and cow pastures of the lowlands. A wan moon was rising and there was a glint of frost on the tussock.

The road opened out again after the closeness of the hills around the pass. A sign flashed past, 'View of Mount Cook.' It seemed stupidly improbable, yet it warned of the white giants that crouched over the indistinct horizon.

Climbing again, until over the rise Lake Tekapo rolled out, palely transfixed between the hills. The moon reflected more brightly off the further ridges; there was a hint of snow and cavernous valleys that ran back to a guarded source in the heart of the mountains. We sped through Tekapo township, meagre yellow lights revealing a jumble of wires, fences and weatherboard. The Church of the Good Shepherd squatted on its headland, blind to the jumble behind, watching the shifting expressions of lake and mountain.

The road flowed away to Irishman Creek and Simon's Hill, an outpost of trees and houses. Now we seemed to be driving to nowhere. The mountains lay distant, the wide tussock basins revealed no limits and time pressed heavily. Our destination was not close enough to stimulate a final burst of effort, and in the small hours of the morning we seemed suspended in a somnolent world.

The road became rougher and more tortuous. Another lake came into view—Pukaki—but still the landscape beyond was inscrutable. The ride was smoothed briefly as we passed over Pukaki dam; then a familiar signpost 'Mt Cook 37'.

There was a faint grey in the sky; the landscape stirred and stark ridges appeared from the blanket of stars. There was no colour with the first light of dawn, only the quality of a grainy photograph, a half-world, unpromising; and a scattering of sheep on the easier hills suggested maggots on the fleshier parts of a gaunt carcase. The milky-grey water of Lake Pukaki stirred with a sudden breeze; ducks and pukeko ruffled their feathers in discomfort; a faint pink trimmed the snow of the peaks to the north.

We rounded a bend. Involuntarily I stopped the car. Unearthly, like an exotic mirage, Mount Cook glowed in the first sunlight, a pink sculpture foursquare between its satellites, floating on a level of its own above the creamy shadows of the lower glaciers. The bulging ice and sheer eastern faces were rounded, smooth and alluring in this uniform pink radiance. The mountain was at once aloof and welcoming, as if to tread its highest slopes would be simple pleasure. It was terrifyingly beautiful; grand in shape yet subtle in texture.

As the broader scene became touched with colour, the mountain shifted into shades of full day: the pink turned to grey and then to an unblemished white, shattering to the eye. We drove into this mountain day, tiredness gone, spirits alive to the shining landscape.

⬥

Few travellers discover Mount Cook at dawn, floating in calm light. More often it is seen in the warmth of a summer afternoon, from a distance, appearing and disappearing, a white massif between the nearer brown hills, meeting Samuel Butler's description in 1860, '. . . towering in a massy parallelogram . . . far above all the others . . . no one can mistake it. If a person says he *thinks* he has seen Mount Cook, you may be quite sure that he has not seen it.'[1]

[1]Samuel Butler, *A First Year in Canterbury Settlement*, London, 1863.

Some will approach without gaining a distant view, as nor'west clouds boil and bank over the ranges. There will be a sense of expectancy, moving from the dry, sunbaked Mackenzie tussock down the side of Pukaki into the cool, gloomy amphitheatre where the Tasman and Hooker valleys meet. There will be no sign of mountains until, impossibly high, a triangle of ice breaks the cloud, the ethereal tip of Aorangi, 'the cloud piercer'. The Maori name is well known, the embodiment of it rare.

At other times acquaintance with Mount Cook will be limited by rain . . . gusty, drenched days: views of battered matagouri bushes, torrents eager to break their banks, waterfalls shooting over bluffs in wild abandon; the only sound, fading and waxing with the blustering wind, the roar of unbridled water; the only smell the bitter aroma of wet rock; the only feeling one of insidious cold, beading the skin with moisture. And one could stay for days at the Hermitage to depart without seeing beyond the thin, bedraggled fingers of snow that drape the valley sides . . . .

Yet it can all be seen in a fast, embracing sweep, flying lazily down the Tasman Glacier, Cook at the window. But this is the approach for the collector of places, not for the traveller who savours landscape.

Travel through the Mackenzie Country is a worth-while preamble to the Mount Cook alpine region. This wide inland basin, never falling below 1000 feet, stretches past and among the outlying arms of mountains that issue from the Main Divide. Eighty miles in length, northeast to southwest, and fifteen to fifty miles wide, it cradles a host of major and minor snow-fed rivers that eventually flow together as the great Waitaki ('weeping waters'), on which the country's biggest earth dam and hydro-electric station are situated. Dams bar the rivers, new lakes have been formed, old lake levels raised, generating electricity for the power-hungry populations of the east coast and North Island. Pylons, like skeletal, petrified giants, are strewn on a landscape where once, aeons ago, acres of ice took the place of powdery blue lakes and swift grey rivers. Evidence of glacial grinding and shaping is still clear—chiselled mountainsides, terraces above the lakes and, as at Pukaki, moraine hillocks adjacent to concrete dams.

There are four easy ways into the Mackenzie Country: by Burkes Pass and by Mackenzie Pass in the east, up the Waitaki Valley in the southeast, and over the Lindis Pass in the southwest. From the earliest times the Maoris frequented all four routes and there is evidence of a heyday of ancient settlement before the pockets of beech forest were reduced and internecine wars decimated the pas at Tekapo and Ohau. But the lovely Maori names persist and myths populate crags and pools.

Tekapo ('preparing to leave in the night') was an appropriate, silent witness to the forays of the first white man to discover the inland tussock basin. It is named after him. James McKenzie[2] stole sheep near Timaru in the 1850s, hid them in the basin, then drove them south on the long inland trail to buyers in Southland. An intrepid Scot and an accomplished sheep drover (aided by a now-legendary dog), he doubtless negotiated the twisting Lindis Pass with his wandering mob. A well-trodden Maori route connecting Central Otago

[2]There are three legitimate spellings of this name: 1. Mackenzie (Country), 2. McKenzie (James), 3. MacKenzie (on Burkes Pass monument).

and the Mackenzie Country, the Lindis is now the highest main highway pass in New Zealand.

The development of the basin for sheep farming followed McKenzie's capture with 1000 stolen ewes just after he had reached his sanctuary. With him safely in jail, his apprehendors capitalised on the sheep stealer's discovery and made applications for the first blocks of land.

Today, in the Church of the Good Shepherd at Tekapo, an inscribed volume records the movements of the men and women who first came to make a home and living on these barren, remote plains.

Pioneers of GLENMORE STATION
(Once Gristhorpe and Castle Hall)
including
MOUNT JOHN and CASS FORKS

| YEAR | RUNHOLDERS | FAMILY AND MANAGERS | STATION HANDS |
|---|---|---|---|
| 1857 } | John Hay (Mount John, 15,000 acres); | | |
| 1858 } | Joseph Beswick (Gristhorpe, | John Evans | |
| 1859 | 28,000 acres) | and his wife | |
| 1860 | ,, ,, | | |
| 1861 | ,, ,, | | |
| 1862 } | Hon. John Hall | | |
| 1863 } | George Hall, Tom Hall | | — McLeod (head |
| 1864 } | (Castle Hall) | | shepherd) |
| 1865 | ,, ,, | | |
| 1866 | ,, ,, | | |
| 1867 | . . . . . . . . | | |

These are plain facts that do not reveal the trials of a harsh climate that can astound with its extremes. In the central Mackenzie Country the rainfall is around twenty inches a year; thirty miles to the northwest in the mountains this amount can fall in a day. Frost is a constant companion for two-thirds of the year and its winter severity is equalled only in parts of Central Otago. Yet the annual total of sunshine hours at Tekapo (2200) is one of the highest in New Zealand. Such vagaries of climate are explained by the dominating wall of mountains in the west. The strong, prevailing northwesterlies break their hearts on the ramparts of the Main Divide, then gasp hot and dry over the Mackenzie to the east coast, often so furious that blinding sandstorms swirl in the riverbeds. Dry skies by day, unprotective stars by night . . .

Today the sheep runs are fenced, mature trees provide windbreaks for the old-established homesteads, telephone wires follow the metalled roads. In 1864, when young Andrew Burnett, late of Leith, looked across to Mount Cook from the station at Simon's Pass, there was nothing but tussock and a one-roomed cob shanty for boundary riders in the shadow of the mountains. With his scant savings Burnett took a lease on the unclaimed land and he and his wife Catherine made a home in the shanty:

'As the children came along at Mount Cook, more rooms were added in the cob until there were six in all. The closest neighbour was at Braemar, nine miles away. There were no roads, no bullocks, no bridges—nothing but a couple of horses to ride. How dull, you may think! By no means. There was the ever-present fear of snows, the rumble of avalanches, the vast panorama of the Southern Alps criss-crossed with those dark venomous gorges that so captivated Samuel Butler and led him to write his great satire *Erewhon*.

'The nearest doctor was 140 miles away at Timaru, and there most of us children were born. Very soon after each child arrived Mother returned to Mount Cook, where, as well as attending to the menfolk, cooking, darning, and making butter, she taught us kiddies.'[3]

The stoic, pioneering spirit of Catherine Burnett is marked by a monument from which one can look south to the alluvial river flats by Lake Pukaki and north to the mountains and their snows which govern the cycle of work on the station. Snow hampers mustering, kills sheep and delays lambing until December. Even now there is an aspect of isolation and brooding harshness about the station, alleviated only by the midsummer sun and trees in full leaf, planted by perhaps the most famous Burnett—'T.D.' Thomas David Burnett was well known to New Zealand at large as a member of Parliament, but he built Mount Cook Station up to the size it is today (30,000 acres) and had a hand in the successful development of other Mackenzie runs. He was something of a mystic and visionary too, as his inscription on the Burkes Pass monument reveals:

> 'O ye who enter the portals of the MacKenzie to found homes, take the word of a child of the misty gorges, and plant trees for your lives: so shall your mountain facings and river flats be preserved to your children's children and for evermore.'

T.D. was a firm but fair boss and the first man he employed on the station at the turn of the century stayed forty years.

'The run in those days was unfenced, and when the snow muster took place every April and the sheep were brought down to safe country, I had to live the winter alone with my dogs at the Golden Gully Hut. Every day I walked the ridges and hunted back sheep trying to make their way up to the high country. . . . the whole winter by myself, out of sight or sound of any living soul.'[4]

The homestead now is replete with memories and mementoes, revealing the tradition and creed of the Burnett family which still owns the great station. The work is still tough, little eased in such country by modern aids. And a new recruit might still be tested by the Burnett code—casually led up a 'short cut' by the boss that turns out to be a beetling bluff, capable of cowing any but the stout-hearted. A pair of boots, a dog, a stick—and anything is possible.

In some respects Andrew Burnett was a late arrival when he established Mount Cook Station in 1864. The run on the western side of Lake Pukaki had been taken up six years

[3]Quote by Donald Burnett sen. (about 1942) in Douglas Cresswell, *Early New Zealand Families*, 2nd series ('Burnett of Mount Cook'), Christchurch, 1956.
[4]ibid, quote by Bill Seymour.



Sheep dog monument,
Lake Tekapo

earlier and the furthermost boundaries of his new land had been investigated by scientists in 1862. Julius von Haast, on a geological survey of Canterbury for the Provincial Council, had found no gold to please his employers but discovered instead mountain scenery that had 'not its equal in the European Alps'. This was to prove the real wealth of the region.

Von Haast and his companions made the first crossing of the notorious Tasman River, as yet an unnamed maze of water skeins twisting through a desert of shingle and boulders. There were quicksands to catch the unwary, deceptive currents and a water temperature like that of running ice. On its western side lay a brief wilderness of spiky matagouri bush and wicked, needle-sharp spaniard grass that sprouted like unshaven stubble on the rocky chin of the great glacier to the north. Von Haast named it Tasman during a tour of exploration that stimulated phrases of inadequate exclamation at the wild grandeur of the pristine mountains and glaciers.

The magnitude and spectacle of his surroundings would have been enhanced by their unknown quality, for every journey is longest when first travelled, every scene grandest when first viewed. Mount Sefton (Maunga Atua to the Maoris, 'mountain of the gods') towered assertively in its leonine crouch, 8000 feet above the junction of the Mueller and Hooker valleys; from the Grand Plateau beneath Mount Cook the Hochstetter Icefall flowed actively to the Tasman Glacier 4000 feet below, a cascade of seracs like a ruin of Christmas icing; the Tasman Glacier itself swept as a broad, white highway, eighteen miles between the shattered ranges, its side roads leading to the ravaged faces and chiselled ridges that fitted into the stark sky like pieces of a jigsaw puzzle.

Scorched by the sun which reflected off the acres of snow, or frozen at night in the vaults of an intrinsically cold and heartless landscape, von Haast found no commercial comfort, only moments of 'extreme delight, never to be forgotten'. His exploration did not start a gold rush but the inner wealth he gained was that which has touched many mountain men since.

The twenty years after von Haast's first visit saw the probings of a handful of explorers and surveyors. Alpine country was only of use to scientists or to those who wished to finish off maps. It is thought that von Haast's party was the first to set foot on the Tasman Glacier but some doubt is cast on this when the story, apocryphal or not, is told of the musterer and the scientist. Climbing high on a misty day in the Mount Cook region, the scientist paused at about 6000 feet to apprise his exhausted companions of the fact that no human being had ever climbed higher in the area. To punctuate his statement, a shout floated down from the mist above. Shortly a panting dog appeared then an unkempt figure with a shepherd's crook. The musterer tipped his hat and said, 'G'day. You jokers seen any sheep on your travels?'

The sheepmen have always been the true pioneers of the high country and their excursions 'all in a day's work' could have led them to first explorations as notable, if less chronicled, as those of their scientific countrymen. Though the icefields hold no attraction for the sheepman, curiosity and a sense of adventure are universal, and who knows who first trod the glaciers and what ridges were first climbed by a lonely musterer?

In 1873 the Governor of New Zealand, Sir George Bowen, visited the Mount Cook area and camped near the site of the present Hermitage Hotel. He saw the tourist possibilities of the region and offered assistance to any member of the English Alpine Club who would attempt the first ascent of Mount Cook. This would be one way of gaining publicity. But nine years passed before anyone took up the challenge of Mount Cook and initiated the sport of mountaineering in New Zealand.

In 1882, over the potholed bullock tracks of Mount Cook Station and the treacherous bed of the Tasman River, a party led by an Irish climber, the Rev. W. S. Green, set out to tackle the unknown mountain. Harried by alpine weather that had already established a notorious reputation, faced by misleading ridges, dazzling icefalls and avalanching faces, they failed in their attempt on the summit by a mere thirty vertical feet. It was a stout effort and proved that Mount Cook was no mean adversary, despite its junior status in height to the peaks of Europe. But Green had found a lower snowline, and the difficulties began earlier—Cook was no junior in other respects.

Green's attempt fired the ambitions of young local men who had learned to live and move among the rough foothills. With little alpine experience and less equipment, they picked up the challenge. The leading member of this group was Christchurch banker G. E. Mannering. He and his companions made five attempts to climb Aorangi between 1886 and 1891.

It was hard, demoralising work to reach even the foot of the mountain, despite the Hermitage Hotel—opened in 1884—which could be used as a base. Trackless moraines, vicious scrub, rough bivouacs and mule-sized loads—all were suffered before the dangerous ice and rocks of a virgin mountain were tackled. '. . . you try to walk, but stagger about like a drunken man; there is no small to your back, your back tendons are puffy and tired like those of an old horse, your head swims, and your eye is dim. . . . But then, you see, we are enjoying what you [European mountaineers] cannot get. Exploring and opening out virgin fields, learning to be our own guides—and porters—from that best of masters—hard experience.'[5]

The Southern Alps demanded a tough exploring instinct; there were no civilised palliatives. Climbing was a matter of individual initiative and labour; there was no support save from one's immediate companions, no reward other than the achievement of exploration despite great physical odds.

Mannering and his companions did not succeed, but their spirit of endeavour spread and sustained the enthusiasm of others. The spur of competition came to the struggle for Cook's summit when another British climber sent notice of intent to carry off the prize in 1895 with the help of a Swiss guide. A Cook veteran, M. J. Dixon, wrote: 'We were of opinion that the top of Aorangi could be reached by a New Zealand party without the help of a guide.'[6] On Christmas Day, 1894, three New Zealand amateur climbers, George Graham, Tom Fyfe and Jack Clarke, reached the summit of Cook, decorating the summit, not with a national flag, but with an old sugar bag.

The hard and straightforward pioneer approach to climbing became characteristic and, though transport and facilities have improved greatly since the 1880s, it still pervades the

[5]G. E. Mannering, *With Axe and Rope in the New Zealand Alps*, London, 1891.
[6]*New Zealand Alpine Journal*, May 1895, p. 9.

sport. It is a sport with no set play and it has never involved more than a minority of the country's population. But a remarkable variety of people from all walks of life have taken to the mountains and through the sport have contributed much to our knowledge of the high country's inner recesses. There is only esoteric merit in knowing well the correct way to climb a particular ice ridge at 10,000 feet—no more than knowing how to kick a ball a given distance between two upright posts. But where the musterer is the intimate of the tussock hills and shingle faces, the mountaineer is the intimate of the snow slopes and rock ridges. Both contribute much to the understanding of the vast expanse of mountain country that dominates the South Island.

Mountaineering grew by fits and starts, with both amateurs and guides participating. In the Mount Cook area their activities, and the activities of all other visitors to the region, were centred on the Hermitage. Tourist interest developed after Green's climb and to cater for this the first Hermitage Hotel was opened in 1884. It was a bold venture, since coach transport had to be provided from the railhead at Fairlie if tourists were to be attracted in numbers. But trade was not brisk and the first private owners went bankrupt, to be bought out by the Government in 1895. Government ownership persisted until 1921, by which time a new hotel had replaced the first, damaged beyond repair by flood in 1913.

The second Hermitage, under the ownership of Rudolph Wigley and his Mount Cook Motor Company between 1921 and 1942, developed a reputation for hospitality and conviviality that has become almost legendary. The hotel operated a professional guiding service that had grown from the early exploits on Mount Cook. Guides mingled with guests of all ages and types, and whether the visitor participated in simple walks, glacier excursions or high climbs something of the lore and substance of the alpine surroundings was imparted to him.

Visits to the Hermitage were more than a two-day whistle stop as part of a package tour of the South Island. People returned year after year to enjoy the atmosphere of a mountain hotel and the relaxing breadth of alpine scenery. The guides persuaded many, in the friendly warmth of the hotel lounge, to undertake the mountain climb or pass trip they had dreamt of but would never have undertaken without such encouragement and inspiration. From these excursions came more satisfaction than could ever be found through the lens of a high-powered telescope or the perspex window of a ski-plane.

The old traditions and atmosphere of a remote mountain hotel and its guides were rapidly lost in the late 1950s. In 1957 the second Hermitage was burnt down, to be replaced by a modern tourist hotel that relinquished tradition for fast-moving trade. Improved communications, especially by air, increased the turnover. Ski-plane flights became a substitute for excursions on foot. At the same time, the Mount Cook National Park was established. Guiding responsibilities passed to its rangers and subsequently the profession died. Now the ordinary person's contact with the mountains is barred or at least conditioned by an efficient hotel itinerary, official board control and the noisy mechanics of modern transport.

Not only the Hermitage has altered in the name of progress. The shadow of material development flickers over every corner of the high country. From a clatter of bulldozers come dams and canals; lake waters rise insidiously to drown the golden tussock and obliterate the links of human tradition; new roads scar the hillsides; cables sway across the ridges. The mountains are used for power and tourism and something of their splendour is lost when the landscape is chiselled and altered to suit economic needs.

Today more people than ever go to the mountains, seeking beauty and peace; but the bare sinews of economics greet them, to dull the joys of their journey. To see and feel these mountains as von Haast did, 'extreme delight, never to be forgotten', one must move past the power lines, begin where roads end, reach out for the still natural hills . . .

We stopped before the icy turret of the peak. Sweat and snow cream had congealed on my nose and the dark goggles bit into my cheekbones; my neck was red from the ice-reflected sun, my shoulders from the rub of pack straps. Pulling out a spike, I knocked it into the ice and secured the rope. With a glance at the others, I stepped up and began cutting at the unmarked curve of dazzling snow that led to the summit. Higher, my head topped a ridge, the wind freshened and my breath caught in my throat as I looked down on a suddenly revealed abyss, full of evil rock and swirling mist. My grip on life seemed tenuous. If I should simply fall . . .

More slowly I began cutting steps up the narrow cone until, near the delicate wafer crest, I shaped a platform from which I could safeguard the others. As I pulled the rope in, they clawed up carefully then paused beneath me on precarious holds. The wind was stronger and our shouts of exultation were lost; but this was no loss—there was no need of words.

I lifted my goggles and looked over the maze of ice and unrestricted wildness of the ridges and chasms. The sea was half hidden by tumbling cloud; in the other direction Lake Pukaki and the Mackenzie Country seemed strangely clear and calm and flat. Mount Cook from the summit was still great but not so selfish in its dominance. It was the cornerpost of mountains far greater in the sum.

I filled my lungs with biting air as the others turned to make their way down. It was good to be alive, to exist within such a primeval scene, to have striven with body and mind through difficulties to a simple end. The all-night drive, the hard tramp with heavy pack that followed, the cold breakfast—these had been hard to bear, but ah, the climax!

Tourists on the Tasman Glacier

Moulin in the Tasman Glacier

National Park ranger, Mount Cook

Tourists at the Hermitage binocular

Hochstetter Icefall and Glacier

*Above* Lake Pukaki

*Below* Lindis Pass hills in winter

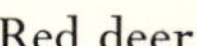

Red deer

Chamois

Shoeing

Merino rams

MOUNT COOK STATION

Preserved notice

Hunters at Kea Point

Church of the Good Shepherd, Lake Tekapo

Pylons near Irishman Creek

Artist, Lake Tekapo

Old dray,
Lake Pukaki

*Above* Mount Cook Station (looking west)

*Below* Lake Tekapo, Church of the Good Shepherd

Nor'west
cloud arch,
winter,
Mackenzie
Country

*Opposite*
*Above* The Upper Tasman Glacier. (Peaks, *left to right:* Mt De la Beche, the Minarets, Mt Elie de Beaumont, Hochstetter Dome, Mt Darwin)
*Below* The Hermitage, with Mt Sefton and the Footstool behind

The Anzacs from Plateau Hut, Grand Plateau

Mount Cook, with Mount Dampier and St David's Dome beneath and Tasman Valley, Lake Pukaki and Mackenzie Country in distance

# ROAD TO THE WEST

## *Arthur's Pass*

For the coach is raising the rolling dust, as hot as Sahara sand,
And the ford is wide, and the steep hill-track is the gate of
    the western land.
It's onward, onward, onward and westward still,
  By the ferny gully and hanging cliff,
  Where the turns are short, and the climbing stiff,
And the horses pull and sweat with a will—
Horses the pride of the western land,
A champion whip with the ribbons in hand;
Life is a jest from the top of the hill,
For the brakes are on, and it's westward still.

FROM 'In the Coach'
BY David McKee Wright



*Overleaf* Chapel at
Arthur's Pass

Open tops on the Bealey Range above Arthur's Pass

# *Road to the West*

WE TRAMPED up the road, gravel scattering from our boots, the steady roar of water an undertone to our clumping rhythm. The noise of our boots changed pitch as we walked across the worn boards of a bridge and below I saw, indistinctly in the dark, a swirl of black water and dashing foam from rapids. A thin moon lit the road and the sickly bush at the edges, dusty and bedraggled from the billowing wake of cars. Heads bowed, we concentrated on a measured pace and sought to avoid the stones and potholes that might disturb it. Time and weather occupied our thoughts and we looked up only to acknowledge another milestone or to watch the small rolls of white cloud coddling the high mountain basins.

As the road climbed higher, the sound of water receded, the forest thinned and the landscape opened into a hilly upland of snowgrass and tussock. We crossed another bridge and came to the monument, a plinth rising incongruously from surrounding boulders and scrub, perpetuating the memory of Arthur Dudley Dobson, who had discovered the pass that lay ahead.

The road stopped climbing and we stood beside a stone that marked an arbitrary demarcation between east and west. Looking back into Canterbury, the mountains spread out and there was a suggestion of river plains beyond the small, yellow lights of the village. Westward the scene was forbidding, with black ranges competing for space and no suggestion of life. The gorge below was filled with cloud, lapping the last rise to the pass, and occasional streamers flowed over to finger the brackish tarns.

It is a reflective time, the hour before dawn, and in the darkness that masked the road it was easy to imagine that we were the only travellers in an unblemished natural world. I thought of the time when this could have been true, when Maoris, singly or in small groups, picked their way across the rough landscape, bound for the western valleys and greenstone—*te pounamu*. A handful of Maori names still grace the rivers of the region, an occasional reminder of the first people to know its mountains and valleys.

But that seemed a remote time, as nebulous as the rising mist at our feet, wrapped in the folds of legend and unwritten history. It was easier to grasp the dates and events of pragmatic Europeans.

There was a soft flutter of wings as two pipits responded to the first promise of dawn. I looked up and a glow in the sky revealed that the sun was coming. My companion had become impatient, so we shouldered our packs and walked down into the cloud.

From the crest of Arthur's Pass it is hard to comprehend the country as Dobson saw it in 1864. He wrote of thick bush, cliffs and gorges and took two days to reach the pass from the Waimakariri River. This has a ring of the incredible when one can drive now from Christchurch to the pass in less than three hours.



Punchbowl waterfall, Arthur's Pass

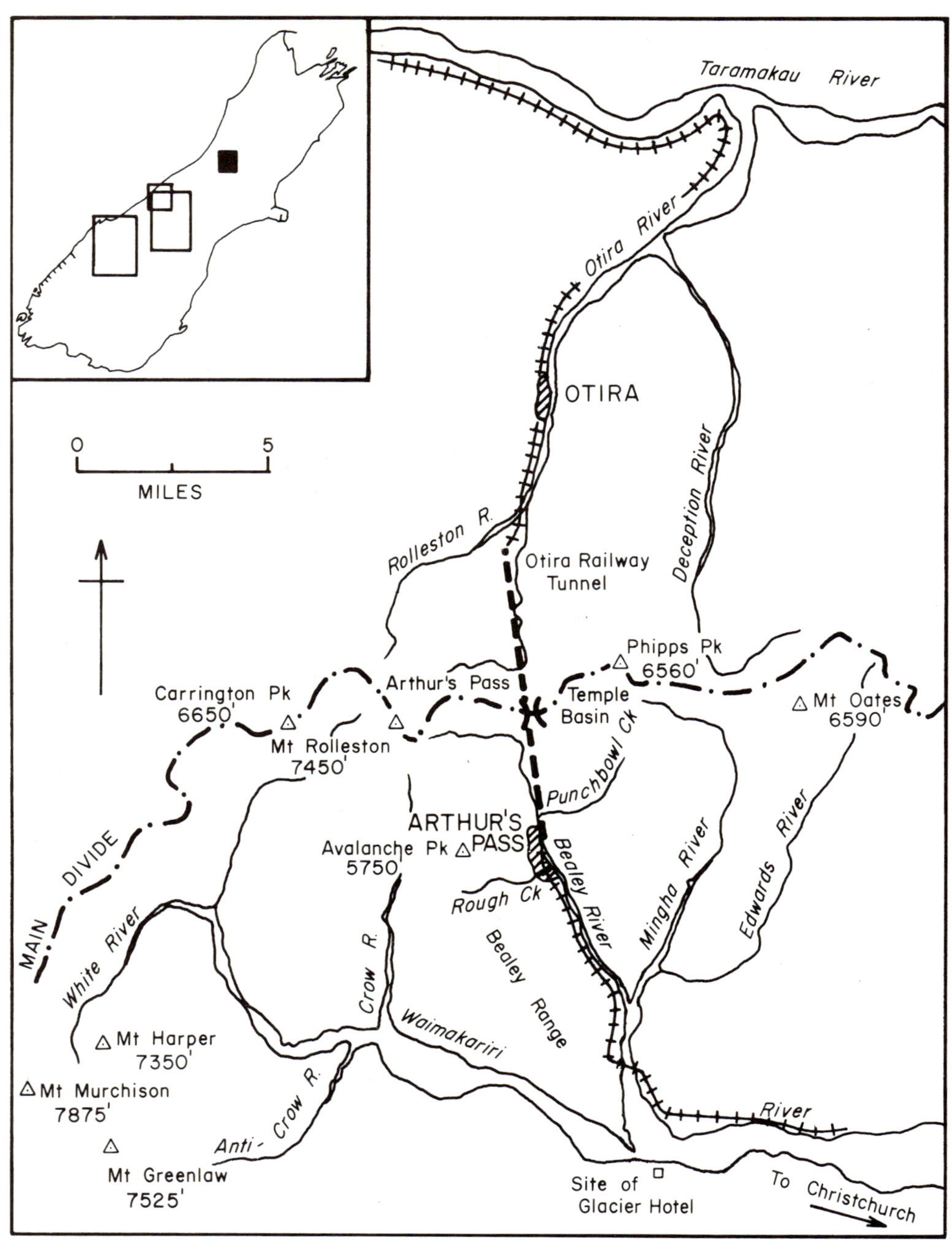


In 1860 Samuel Butler wrote, 'The back country of the Waimakariri is inaccessible by dray' and told of alpine grandeur. But—'How one does long to see some signs of human care in the midst of the loneliness! How one would like, too, to come occasionally across some little *auberge*, with its *vin ordinaire* and refreshing fruit!'[1]

Perhaps he would have regretted the 'signs of human care' that are plain more than a century later: a road scars the hillsides, ugly power pylons break the line of tumbling

[1]Samuel Butler, *A First Year in Canterbury Settlement*.

beech forest; chamois track the snow; deer eat the seedlings and opossums strip the leaves; erosion savages the mountains, feeding more dross to the milky rivers. Human care has been mostly conspicuous by its absence; and there is no *auberge*, no *vin ordinaire*, to ease the traveller.

Yet for all the scars, the mountains and valleys of Arthur's Pass and the Waimakariri River ('wintry cold water') can still stir the traveller's heart; from the first vista of the Waimakariri peaks, to the rainbow spray of unchanged waterfalls and the pressing domination of high peaks above the village, huddled in the narrow Bealey Valley that runs down from the pass.

It is a region of marked contrasts that has attracted visitors since the end of World War I, increasingly so with improved access by road and rail. The establishment of reserves at the turn of the century and a national park in 1929 has ensured a measure of control and planned development, so that now it is one of the finest recreational areas in the country. There is bush for the naturalist and hunter, snow and rock for the mountaineer, high basins for the skier, graded tracks, alpine gardens and a museum for the tourist. The Waimakariri watershed is well known and every valley has its tracks and huts; though still wild alpine country, it provides an ideal proving ground for those who would begin to learn about and enjoy the varied nature of mountains.

European interest and development of the area began with Arthur Dobson; an engineer-surveyor for the Canterbury Provincial Government, he was sent to locate a pass to the West Coast at the head of the Waimakariri. He fulfilled his brief in March 1864, later confirming from the west that his pass at the head of the Waimakariri tributary he called the Bealey (after the reigning Superintendent of Canterbury) connected with the Otira River which joined the Taramakau. His discovery caused little excitement and even Dobson was doubtful about his pass's use for a road. But the gold rush to the West Coast, which began soon after his survey, vastly changed the significance of the pass. It was soon established that 'Arthur's pass was the best route' to the goldfields and there followed feats of road engineering to be wondered at even now.

Within a year hundreds of men with pick and shovel hacked a coach road from the gorges and river beds to form a link between east and west that served the needs of a gold-digging population that grew to 28,000 by 1867. In March 1866 a regular coach service began and for £8 one could sample the scenic wonders of a South Island crossing from Christchurch to Hokitika. But it was a 36-hour, bone-jarring journey fraught with danger if the rivers flooded (there were thirteen major crossings), or if the lever brake showed signs of slipping on the hectic descent down the Otira Gorge.

The prospect of gold brought urgent human activity to a highland that was unknown and unnamed only two years before. Men toiled with pick and axe at the stubborn rock and tough bush, shaping a highway through a landscape that had lain undisturbed for millenia; men tramped grimly through snow at the 3000-ft crest of the pass in winter, or baked in midsummer sun, toting swags that contained little more than their dreams of a fortune. They came from all over New Zealand and Australia and even further afield; in one week in October 1865 more than 500 men went over the pass in their spring fever.

Gold, and its attendant trade and services, made Westland alive and cut a way through mountains previously thought impassable. Cobb and Co's coach line built up a reputable and dependable service and along its route a variety of hotels and staging posts sprang up. Perhaps the best known was the Glacier Hotel at the Bealey Corner where a fordman was posted to guide coaches across the unbridged Waimakariri: once a party of four Maoris spent four days marooned in the middle of the river when their coach became stuck and they declined rescue on horseback.

Hair-raising tales abound from the old coaching days, though there were few fatalities during those fifty-seven years. This was probably due as much to the instinct and strength of the horses as to the legendary skill of the drivers. . . . 'The snow had stopped falling, but there was a thick white fog—one couldn't see anything, not even the horses in the lead. . . . We pulled up at the bottom of the cutting . . . and discussed the position. Clarke said, "There's only one thing to do, put out the lights, which do us no good and only confuse the horses. They know the road, so we'll let them take us over." I have every confidence in Clarke but . . . I was precious glad when we found ourselves safely over that dangerous cutting of several miles, where we should have dropped three or four hundred feet into the river had the horses blundered.'[2]

On another occasion a driver fell asleep (with the encouragement of whisky on a cold night) while his coach was descending the Otira Gorge. The single passenger suffered a gruelling ride that often went close to disaster. Not until arrival at the Otira Hotel did he discover that—though the sleeping driver's foot had been jammed on the brake—only the exhausted horses had taken them down safely.

In the first years of its existence the coach line ran from Christchurch to Hokitika, leaving the Canterbury capital at about 4 a.m. one day, reaching the West Coast town at 9 p.m. on the next. In fits and starts the railway took over parts of the route. In 1880 the line from Christchurch to Springfield, at the edge of the foothills, was opened and in 1883 a royal commission came out in favour of the Arthur's Pass route for the West Coast railway. But it was 1900 before the western section as far as Otira was opened and 1906 before tenders were called for the construction of a tunnel from the present site of Arthur's Pass village to Otira. The whole project was delayed by political argument, the decline of goldmining on the Coast and the claims of alternative routes.

Completion of the tunnel took fifteen years. The first shot was fired at Otira in 1908 but after two years only one of the five and a third miles had been excavated. The rock proved crumbling and dangerous, and up to 3000 gallons of water a minute seeped down from the mountains above to hamper work. Yet, despite the atrocious working conditions, only one man lost his life, through rockfall.

The original contractor gave up the job in 1912 and the Government took over; but work was further delayed by the onset of war. By 1914 the railway line from Christchurch had been extended as far as the tunnel entrance in the Bealey Valley and the coach line was reduced to a ferry service between there and Otira. The heavy coaches with their big hickory wheels and iron 'tyres' made their last trip in 1923. The only reminders of those romantic pioneering days are a single coach preserved in the Arthur's Pass museum and the occasional sight of old cuttings below the present motor road.

[2]A. P. Harper, *Memories of Mountains and Men*, Christchurch, 1946.

With the start of tunnelling, Arthur's Pass village was born. Work huts and shanties were flung up on the Bealey River flats and when tunnel work was completed many were taken over privately for use as holiday baches. The construction site remained a focus for settlement, for railway yards were built for holding wagons which were ferried through the tunnel by electric locomotives. A regular rail service stimulated recreational development in the Arthur's Pass area; a hostel was opened, day trips became popular and the first skis were used there in the winter of 1927.

Mountain enthusiasts began to appreciate the opportunities that existed in the largely unexplored ranges that now lay within a few hours' train journey of Christchurch. G. N. Carrington, a lad of eighteen, publicised the beauties of the Waimakariri mountains and was the key figure in the formation of the Christchurch Tramping Club in 1925. This later became the Canterbury Mountaineering Club and its members were instrumental in opening up the region for climbing and tramping. Skiing interests were not far behind and in 1929, the year the national park was created, the Christchurch Ski Club was formed.

From this time, despite limitations imposed by depression and war, the region embraced by the national park was developed or preserved for the people. Arthur's Pass village became the centre of activity, the halting point for thundering steam locomotives and, later, diesel railcars; the road was slowly transformed from a largely unbridged shingle track to a sealed motor road; stores opened and club huts were built. In recent years the shanty town aspect of railway huts has been improved by the addition of homes and buildings constructed from local stone. Now Arthur's Pass is the only truly alpine village in the Southern Alps, with a small permanent population and a traditional atmosphere that is lacking in other tourist resorts.

Perhaps the village is most picturesque in winter, when snow mantles the scree and stark rock of the peaks that loom over the valley; when it powders the bush and waterfalls freeze into festoons of icicles. Cottage roofs become heavy with blankets of snow that shift in the brief hours of sunlight and curl wetly over the gutters.

Once I watched a whole winter pass from the wide windows of a village cottage half buried in snow drifts and sheltered by the coarse but resilient evergreen branches of beech trees. Through the short days, life was governed by the shifting line of sunlight as it blazed on the summits in the morning then slowly moved over the dark trees to briefly warm the crusted snow flecked with splinters of firewood at my door.

It was a lonely time, with rare company, and life was a simple ritual, moving with sun-warmth and cold; the tempo of dripping icicles told the time of day and only the occasional noise of trains punctuated the indefinite hours of night. A journey outside meant boots, sweaters and a trudge through slushy road-snow to the store for food and news of an outside world that seemed prosaic and distant, unchanged and unaffected by the absence of my day-to-day concern in the city.

If there was a lack of human company, there was no lack of flying friends, who grew to know that mine was one of the few occupied cottages. Chaffinches, tits and grey warblers graced the branches near the windows and appeared at regular times in a cycle of searching for food. But one day as I sat writing, gazing out at the bitter rain that had come to thrash the old snow, a face appeared, upside down, peering inquisitively through the top of the window. Droplets of water ran down this incorrigible kea's bill and splashed against the glass as he cocked his head. Feathers bedraggled and ruffled against the rain and cold, his insatiable curiosity overcame the obvious discomforts of weathering a nor'west storm on the gutter.

Moved to pity some nights later, I put food in the snow for this kea and his family, which had no doubt bullied me into this by sitting on the roof each crack of dawn to screech and natter until I was awake. Moving clumsily over the snow to their food, they waddled and slid, stopping to throw back their heads and screech so that with their long beaks they looked like trumpeting elephants. They were unafraid, cocky, nosy and mischievous. Wandering into the cottage in search of more food, or to sample the lino with a swift wrench of their wicked beaks, they had to be treated like naughty children; with a not-too-heavy boot I bundled them into the cold evening, their feathers ruffling in outrage.

Keas are the true natives of the mountains, breeding under subalpine rocks, hovering and tumbling in a mass of scarlet and green on the eddies of alpine winds, climbing cautiously up steep snow, their claws acting as crampons, heads bent forward so that beaks can be used as tiny ice axes. For every mountaineer they are familiar companions and often the drudgery of ploughing through deep snow or fighting against wind and rain is alleviated by a sudden 'keee-ya' from a distant ridge: one bird sees the lumbering climber, calls his clan, and spirits are lifted as they circle and shriek overhead.

They have a reputation for destruction and are reviled as pests; but a unique animal curiosity, more than a savage purpose, causes them to examine and pull apart any object alien to their barren landscape. One can be glad that their revilers are limited in number, that the tough bird has outstayed the depredations of humanity and remains securely in charge of a territory that is not man's.

The keas were company in a village winter and so were the few people who lived there the year round. The lone storekeeper stocked goods to meet any demand, whether for coal or gumboots, meat or newspapers, clothes or fruit. Though prices could not compete with those of the days of tunnel-driving, the store was a warm place for gossip about the weather or skiing prospects at Temple Basin.

The first store in the village opened to serve the tunnellers over sixty years ago. It is recorded that, 'Wages were low, but so were prices. The luxuries were chocolate, lollies, tobacco—"Havelock 10*d*" and "cigs 6*d*". Half a pound of tea cost 10*d*; a pound of mutton 5*d*; a pound of butter 1*s* 3*d*; and a pound of salt 1*d*.'[3] A pair of long underpants or an axe cost 6*s*, a mattress 13*s* 6*d* and a pack of cards 1*s*. I had no need for long underpants or a mattress but the store was always a welcome sight, winter or summer—especially at the end of a hot and tiring day of climbing. I would look for it from high on the mountainsides, my energy sustained by the thought of ice cream and a billyful of milk at journey's end.

One evening as I walked back from the store a car swept through the soft snow in chains,

[3]Grace Adams, *Jack's Hut*, Wellington, 1968.



*Opposite* The Cobb and Company coach in Arthur's Pass museum

COBB & Co

and it was hard to believe that in the days of heavier snowfall it was possible to ski all the way from Arthur's Pass to Otira—acres of unblemished snow, skiers with skins climbing to the crest of the pass then swooping down an Otira Gorge frozen and white. I stopped and looked up towards the pass as the dusk gathered quickly; there was a suggestion of car lights on the winding road through the bush. Beyond the white faces of the Goldney Ridge of Mount Rolleston, there were the heads of clouds in Westland and a brisk northerly breeze rocked the overhead lights near the station. There was little movement now as the cold grew more intense but a touch of warmth came from the glow of softly-lit windows scattered up the valley. I thought that if one could feel entirely at home in the mountains it was here. Turning, I walked on to the promise of a log fire and my company of keas.

⬩

The two dominant features of the Arthur's Pass region are mountains and rivers; the greatest of these, Mount Rolleston and the Waimakariri. Rolleston's ice feeds the source of the river which goes on to slash the cultivated chequerboard of the Canterbury Plains. Sheep dot the lower mountain flats of tussock and matagouri, but the upper reaches have been the preserve since the 1920s of young explorers who have found their first footing in snow and inspiration in the high peaks. 'Mountains came to mean much more than citadels placed in rows merely for the conquest of guided parties and the admiration of passing trampers. The citadels became objects of inspiration and solace, familiar and adventurous territory.'[4]

Those words will have the feel of truth for many mountaineers who made their first forays in the Waimakariri. My own first encounter with mountains was a vision of spring snow sparkling on a clear night on that river's peaks, a sight still vivid in memory, like any scene or event that moulds one's life. Bewitched and humbled at the same time, I became a child of the mountains and nothing seemed more virtuous or valuable than to explore and understand the face of a high landscape.

In the Waimakariri I learnt to ford turbulent streams, to seek a way over shattered rock with unsure hands, to fashion a path through snow with unfamiliar tools. The climbing rope brought friendship, the bivouacs and huts an ability to live simply. And the peaks brought the crystallisation of growing strength and confidence, the slow welding of a bond between myself and the mountains, and an understanding of both.

Those early journeys were full of trepidation when dangers loomed larger than they were. Exhaustion and despair always lay in wait and the toughening of nerve and muscle was no easy task. There were many failures, successes briefly snatched through wind and rain, but sometimes the just reward of effort and perseverance. . . .

⬩

I had chosen a difficult way and became angry as my ice axe jammed on the rock and grazed the back of my hand. Ivan was not to be seen and I shouted with a forced note of con-

[4]John Pascoe, *Unclimbed New Zealand*, London, 1939.

fidence to see if he was ahead or behind. There was no answer. I looked down at the shattered ravines, the ravaged mountainside of scree, and there was no sign of life, as if I were completely alone, stranded on this awkward pinnacle.

With a gasp of annoyance I struggled on and, to my relief, found that I could climb on to an easy spur and a basin of snow. From there, I looked up and saw Ivan nonchalantly plugging up the last slope to the pass, the splash of colour in his shirt both incongruous and reassuring.

When I joined him, red in the face from exertion and chagrin at my bad route-finding, we spread our parkas on the snow and sat down to chew some chocolate. One way we looked into Westland where the inevitable cloud cast dappling shadows on the never-ending jungle; the other way we looked down the wide shingle bed of the Waimakariri, meandering, 'wintry, cold water', binding together jumbled acres of boulders and pebbles. A tiny square of orange in the beech forest marked the hut we had left that morning.

Time was slipping away. It was already 10 a.m. and we wished to climb graceful Carrington Peak above our heads, return to the hut, then tramp sixteen miles to the station at Arthur's Pass in time to catch the train to Christchurch at 8.30 p.m. The chances were slim of climbing the peak and catching the train in the time left. Which was more important, the demand to meet the routine of paper and pen on a city Monday morning or completing our first ascent of this glittering mountain on a spring day full of sun and freedom?

We strapped on crampons and eagerly climbed a rising ramp of snow, tying on the rope when the snow merged with a buttress near the peak—where a fall would have ended at the foot of bluffs a thousand feet below. Soft snow slid away like sago as we pressed on, drawn by the sharp lifting lines of the ridge to the summit.

At a small saddle on the ridge we dropped our packs for the final climb. With a youthful zest that took little stock of danger, we soared up the ridge, crampons biting into the snow, scratching on rock, until we came to the shapely cone of the summit. Cloud had thickened from the west to smother all the surrounding peaks and we seemed to stand on the highest peak on earth as we looked down on a sea of rolling white—cloud and snow broken by occasional shadows of dark valleys utterly remote from our own high vista of sky and sun. It was a vivid moment, too brief in the experience, too soon dulled in the memory.

The descent became more and more of an anticlimax as exhilaration faded and the tiredness from an early morning start and undisciplined climbing overtook us. We reached the hut with the despair of knowing that our day's effort was by no means ended. We had been on our feet for eight hours already and now we faced the task of reaching the station, sixteen miles away, in five hours at the outside. I looked at the hut bunks which invited rest, at the stove which suggested food and comfort, at the patch of sunlit moss and grass outside the door which promised langour. Spirit and flesh were weak.

As we finished packing our loads Ivan mixed a drink which he assured me would revive our energies. It consisted of vodka, grape juice, lots of water and spoonfuls of sugar. I took two aspirins for good measure in a wild experiment and scarcely noticed the soreness of my shoulders as I swung on the pack.

With conviction we slammed the hut door and trotted over the flat, through the trees and down the bank that led to the river bed. There were springs in our heels and wings on our backs as we dashed down the valley, boulder-hopping with consummate ease and skill, never a false step, forging through the river in a shower of water, intent that every step should be longer or faster than before.

A nor'west breeze came from behind to spur us on, and with it a scud of grey cloud and skiffs of rain to cool our perspiring faces. Down valley an enormous rainbow curved from range to range like a triumphal arch. With the air and determination of athletes, we rushed on without pause.

After less than three hours we reached the Arthur's Pass road and eleven of our sixteen miles were behind; two hours remained before the train left. With satisfaction, and building strong hopes of hitching a ride over the last dreary miles of undulating gravel road, we tramped on at an easy pace, pausing often to look back for a telltale cloud of dust or cock an ear for the distant hum of an engine.

But the evening was silent save for the murmur of the Bealey River and the thrashing of treetops in the freshening nor'wester. More miles passed beneath our feet and each new rise in the road dragged at our dwindling reserves of energy. It was galling to walk along an empty road beside a railway line with faint hope of transport, feet burning, eyes gritty, shoulders stiff and numb.

Without warning there was the noise of a car and a flash of lights in the trees as it rounded the bend. Croaking with joy we waved our ice axes and waited for the reassuring sound of brakes and a gear change. But in a moment we were left with a blurred impression of shining metal and glaring lights, and with a cloud of dust on which we choked as we cursed.

At the last bridge before the village Ivan called for a rest, but with the almost certain knowledge that once stopped I would never start again, I trudged on, mere habit placing one foot in front of the other. Ten minutes before the train was due we slumped on to a hard bench and stared at the railway tracks. The memory of standing on Carrington Peak that morning seemed a figment of the imagination, a dream.

Through a haze of fatigue I watched the railcar emerge from the tunnel and pull into the station. The noise seemed clamorous, breaking my torpor with a hiss of brakes, banging of doors and a burst of cheerful voices. The mountain air to which we were addicted was laced by diesel fumes and the smell of humanity in the overheated carriages. Our mountain adventure, our all-consuming enterprise, was finished and the dream of Carrington Peak began to dissipate as the railcar pulled away.

I peered through a window clouded with condensation as the mountainsides rushed past, and for a time I could see the night-dark spaces of the Waimakariri Valley. With a sense of comfort I sank into the cushioned seat; with a sense of regret I passed from a world of simple design and reality to the theatre of human condition.



Otira Gorge

Railcar from Christchurch on Rough Creek bridge, Bealey Valley

*Below* Store and road west, Arthur's Pass

Beech
forest
in late
afternoon
sunlight

Winter special at Arthur's Pass station

Oscar Coberger, craftsman and Pass identity

A milestone from the coaching days

A novice in the hills

Children at play by the chapel

Summer holiday reading

Chalet restaurant

Taking a spell in the Waimakariri Valley

*Opposite*
*Above* Late winter in the Crow Valley; Mt Rolleston behind

*Below* Mountaineers back from the hills: Waimakariri Valley, Mt Harper left background

Waimakariri Valley

# ASPIRING COUNTRY

## *The Matukituki*

In winter blind with snow; but in full summer
The forest blanket sheds its cloudy pollen
And cloaks a range in undevouring fire.
Remote the land's heart: though the wild scrub cattle
Acclimatised, may learn
Shreds of her purpose, or the taloned kea.

For those who come as I do, half-aware,
Wading the swollen
Matukituki waist-high in snow water,
And stumbling where the mountains throw their dice
Of boulders huge as houses, or the smoking
Cataract flings its arrows on our path—

For us the land is matrix and destroyer
Resentful, darkly known
By sunset omens, low words heard in branches . . .

FROM 'Poem in the Matukituki Valley'
BY James K. Baxter

Fallen beech,
West Matuki-
tuki Valley

On Cattle Flat Station

Rob Roy in winter from French Ridge

# Aspiring Country

FROM the beeches we walked out on to Pearl Flat, a name embodied in the glitter of the thinly flowing river and the pale shine of translucent ice patches filling the hollows between tussock and boulder. It was set narrowly in the valley, crowded by competitive spurs that stood almost upright, feet in the river, shoulders rapidly clear of trees as they climbed into snow or broken rock. It was the winter of a big snow and in the Matukituki trees lay in heaps, harvested by avalanche, and the tussock was still hidden, or bent and flattened by the snow as if the river had run over the flats. Fresh falls were scattered on the upper tiers of forest, dissipating in the spare sunlight; cascading streams had shrunk to icicles.

It was easy to cross the river as it dribbled through the boulders from its frozen source and there was comfort in dry boots as we contemplated the climb ahead to the vast winter snowfields on French Ridge. Our packs were heavy with clothes and fuel, for there was no hope of natural warmth displacing the intrinsic cold of August, and the margin between safety and danger was slight.

Despairingly I looked at the narrow track that began at the cairn. It led gently into the first trees and then turned up the abrupt hillside in a maze of projecting roots and branches that formed a steep, uneven ladder. I looked for signs that higher the angle would ease, the track become clearer, but there were none—nothing but the prospect of hard labour.

Grimly absorbed in the effort of climbing through the forest, I felt the world shrink within the compass of the nearer trees with their endless pattern of dull bark, lustreless foliage, saturated roots and moss. My mind was bent on nothing more than the careful employment of muscle and lung. David was stronger than I and sometimes he went out of sight as he moved more quickly, following the blazes that had become the only sign of a track.

The direct line of the track caused us to gain height quickly, and I stopped with a sense of surprise and satisfaction to look through a rare break in the trees and note how far below lay the river and flats. There was a deeper chill in the air and small drifts of old snow littered the ground beneath the beeches. Further up, the trees shrank at the barrier of height and cold and the track became more sharply defined as a line of thick snow through the dwarfed trees. Our progress faltered as we sank thigh deep or fell into holes obscured by the shroud of snow; whole bushes were hidden, their presence revealed only by a misplaced boot or the lurch of an unbalanced body. I looked longingly towards the higher rocks and unblemished snow that marked the end of growth.

The clean-cut lines of the open snow ridge brought relief to strained muscles. Here the footing was sure in clean, compacted snow. But the easier going was accompanied by mounting apprehension, as a fluttering icy wind dashed past, scattering pockets of loose snow. Gloomy billows of mist descended on the peaks which masked Aspiring. Earlier that day we had stretched out in the tussock of the lower valley and watched southwest cloud scudding over the face of the great peak. But we had been lulled into a mood of hope and



At Hell's Gates,
entrance to
West Matukituki

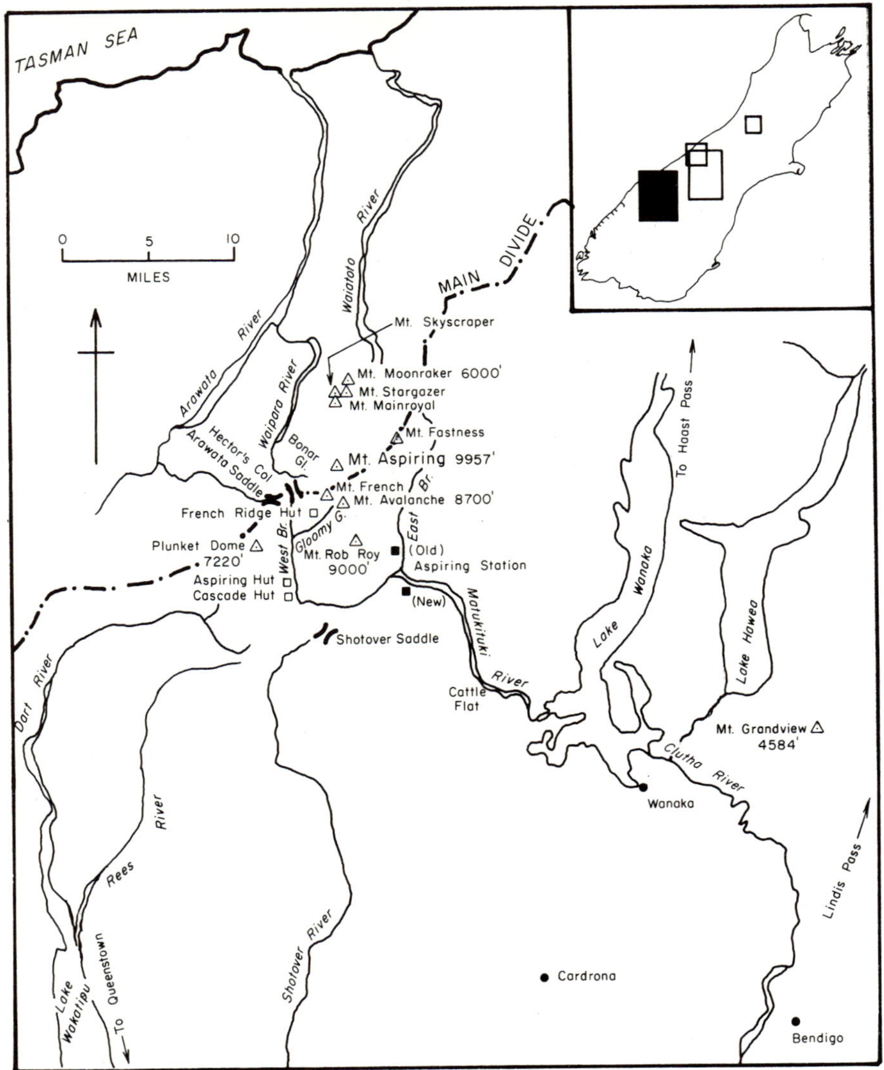


security by the warmth of the sun and the still air of the sheltered flats. Now the weather was breaking over our heads at the midpoint of our journey. We must either go back to the valley, down the tortuous track, or force on through the snow to the hut at 5000 feet. The latter still seemed preferable. We could not bring ourselves to give up the height we had won so laboriously.

At first the sharp wind was stimulating after the dank forest; my cheeks began to glow and I watched with fascination as little whirls of snow twisted down the side of the ridge, ending as slowly-falling puffs of powder as they blew out over the bluffs. There was still a chance that the bad weather would pass over. The cloud parted frequently on the peaks, revealing faces of frost-ravaged rock or balustrades of crevassed ice, and the sun broke through to illumine summits that pierced the cloud like rocks in a tumbling sea. Patches of light travelled swiftly over the mountainside bringing sudden texture to the featureless expanse of snow.

But the sun grew weaker, appearing less and less, until it was lost in a heavy bank of grey cloud that smothered all the higher ridges and slowly sank towards us. Thin skeins of white cloud drifted across the grey at a faster pace and with them came a renewed force in the wind.

Soon not even our steady plod with heavy packs could sustain bodily warmth. We stopped and quickly pulled on extra sweaters, windproofs, mitts and balaclavas, until only our noses and cheeks were exposed. Snow began to fall in showers of large, damp flakes, encrusting our goggles. The cloud finally descended to mask the ridge ahead.

We climbed on urgently, breasting every rise with an extra spurt in the hope of seeing the hut loom out of the cloud. But every blank view brought an extra twinge of anxiety and the higher we climbed the more exposed we became to the increasing waves of wind from the southwest.

Now it was impossible to tell if fresh snow was falling, as the wind picked up drifts and threw them in sheets over the ridge. Increasingly we were forced to stop, ram our axes into the snow and lean into vicious gusts. Fine snow forced its way into our nostrils and through the vents of our goggles into our eyes. The cold surged through my clothing and for an instant I gave way to a sense of fearful menace. As I took in the whole hostile scene—bowing my head to the flying snow, bending my shoulder to the wind—the dividing line between warm life and frozen immobility was briefly obscured. My self-confidence and sufficiency suddenly seemed as nothing against the elements threatening to overwhelm me.

David shouted and my alarm gave way to relief as I caught the exultation in his voice, though his words were carried away by the wind. He waved his ice axe in the air and when I had struggled to his side I could see the dim orange glow ahead—the hut, upright and secure in a world of moving cloud and snow. He plunged on, shouting about hot tea and sleeping bags, but I stood a moment longer, looking around me with a new-found freedom—the joy of escaping from an almost overpowering danger. The sheer oppression of the storm had gone and I could revel in the spectacle of swirling cloud and flying snow, breathing lungfuls of biting air. I ploughed the last few yards to the hut door and knocked the snow from my boots.

In Maori legend the lakes of Hawea and Wanaka were dug by the chief Te Rakaihaitu who had arrived with his followers in the *Uruao* canoe. With his long *ko*, he carved out basins for the deep waters and built mountains from the spoil. Wanaka might mean 'wide unbounded region', describing a scene of cold, blue waters, yellow and green hills and distant ranges of snow mountains where one peak stands out, Tititea, the 'upright glistening mountain'. And the river that flows to Wanaka from the west was called Matukituki, 'the white destroyer', reminding all who travelled in its valley of its power and treachery.

Maoris knew of the Matukituki's main source in its west branch, and of the ice-free saddle which leads to the Arawata headwaters and the West Coast. It is even thought that, twenty-five miles inland from the lake, there was once an encampment on the tussock flats near the present Cascade Hut. But when Europeans explored the South Island interior in the 1850s there were few Maoris near the great lakes; most had moved to the coast for trade with the Pakeha, and the land awaited rediscovery.

The first European to see Lake Wanaka might have been James McKenzie in 1852, the sheep stealer (see p. 20), making his clandestine way south with flocks for sale in Otago and Southland. If he did, he held his tongue, taking silent stock of fine sheep country around the lake basins and down the Clutha River. Young Nathaniel Chalmers probed into Central Otago with Maori guides at about the same time, but the area was not 'officially' discovered until the end of 1857.

J. T. Thomson, Chief Surveyor for the Otago Provincial Government, 'discovered' McKenzie's pass in the north which he called Lindis, and from the Grandview Range further west looked out to Wanaka and Hawea. To the northwest was 'a glorious pyramid of ice and snow' which he named in an inspired moment, Mount Aspiring; this was the Maori Tititea. Other surveyors followed Thomson. Two pushed up the Matukituki, then climbed a peak for a view to the west; their labour and discomfort on this climb prompted a second inspired christening—Mount Perspiring.

Soon there were men in search of gold or leases for millions of acres of grazing land. Access to the region improved and population increased as gold strikes and rushes sprouted from the Lindis to the Shotover, from Bendigo to Cardrona. Enterprising and shrewder men took control of the land from the river beds to the very foot of the Main Divide, burning, felling, cutting, making a way for wool.

The Government explorers surveying the land for its proper administration were barely one step ahead and it is difficult to separate fact from myth, to decide whether surveyors or prospectors reached the valley heads first. And when James McKerrow in 1862 went to map the land around Lake Wanaka, he was met by entrenched runholders who resented his appearance, fearing that the land, once surveyed, would be cut up and divided among new settlers.

For McKerrow, mapping was less exciting than exploration and in March he set out to solve the riddle that plagued his superiors and teased his own imagination—the whereabouts of a pass to the West Coast. The Haast Pass, beyond the head of Lake Wanaka, was still unknown and McKerrow's hopes—which J. T. Thomson's map seemed to support—lay in the West Matukituki.

McKerrow's party found no pass but discovered the glories of a valley which in later years has been described as the most beautiful in the Southern Alps. McKerrow was deeply impressed: 'The thunder of the avalanches is frequently heard; and its overwhelming force displayed in its ruthless track cleft through the forest, where remains of the great trees lie torn and snapped into matchwood. Glacier Dome and Mount Aspiring, enthroned in perpetual ice, bid defiance to the sun and forbid the approach of the beholder, who is spellbound, impressed with awe and veneration at the stupendous forces of nature.'[1]

McKerrow was followed into the West Matukituki the next summer by James Hector

[1]Irvine Roxburgh, *Wanaka Story* (Otago Centennial Historical Publications), Christchurch, 1957.

who, though only twenty-eight, was the holder of a gold medal from the Royal Geographical Society for his explorations in North America. With great determination and resource he led his party to the head of the river and forced a route over a high saddle at 5000 feet to the Waipara and Arawata rivers. They took two days to cross the saddle, climb down the other side 'like flies on a wall', and traverse the glaciers that flowed down from Aspiring. Their provisions dwindling, they pushed on down the Waipara and then the Arawata to a point about fifteen miles from the coast. Here they were forced to turn back. By that time meals consisted of what could be scavenged from the bush, or even less—'With a little tea and a consoling pipe we endeavoured to sleep off appetite.'[2]

The return trek to Otago was hindered by foul weather and floods and their meagre food caches had been plundered by rats. With their stamina strained to the utmost they recrossed what is now known as Hector's Col and regained the supplies and horses left in the Matukituki nearly three weeks before.

Hector's experiences dispelled hopes of a convenient pass from the Matukituki to the West Coast. He had missed the easier Arawata Saddle, a few miles to the southwest, but all passes from the Matukituki led to torn glaciers, broken mountains and impenetrable bush. Sixty-seven years passed before a mountaineering party retraced Hector's route and completed his line of exploration to the sea.

The Matukituki Valley offered no line for a road to the west and, though prospectors found traces of gold in the river, there was not enough to start a rush. The valley was remote from the main settlements and its beauty alone did not attract industry. By the mid-1870s most of the sheep stations around lakes Wanaka and Hawea were well established and the frenzied panning for gold along the Clutha and its tributaries had given place to syndicated dredging and sluicing. Not until this time did settlers move into the Matukituki.

For about fifteen years, from 1876, a sawmilling industry flourished and timber was extracted from the valley as far up as the lower reaches of the east and west branches. Concurrently, leases were taken out for sheep runs: Cattle Flat Station was established in the main valley and Glenfinnan, which stretched to the junction of the two branches. But both the flooding river and that other destroyer, the big winter snow, savaged the flocks. The hold on the land was always tenuous. In the harsh winter of 1878 the snow lay four feet deep for four months and Glenfinnan lost all but one thousand of its nine thousand sheep. Farming under such conditions was a crushing experience and Glenfinnan was abandoned for some years.

The first known settler on the flats beyond the junction of the west and east branches was Hugh McPherson, who built a homestead and ran a few cattle on land that was to become part of the Mount Aspiring Station. The isolation of McPherson and his family was complete when the Matukituki rose. Their access to the rough cart track which meandered thirty miles to the settlement at Wanaka was constantly hampered by a shifting ford through the river that dictated the pattern of life and death. One night, as Hugh McPherson drove home from Wanaka, he fell asleep drunk in his dray, and the horses plodded on, following the track so faithfully that they towed the dray over a bank which the river had

[2]Expedition report by J. W. Sullivan, *Otago Daily Times* (1863).

scoured away. The next day one horse was found standing alone in the freezing water, tied by its traces to the wreckage.

Stoically, McPherson's wife stayed on at the remote homestead, assisted by her husband's brother, Duncan, who later set up his own home in the West Branch. Still on the 'wrong' side of the river, Duncan McPherson's rough house was shadowed by the mountains which rose to 7000 feet from his back door. In winter there was no sun until the middle of the day and snow covered the nearby shingle fans of creeks that carved through the beech forest to the river. The river and the creeks, a constant drum of pounding water that grew to a crescendo in the spring melt . . . 'Mrs McPherson explained to me that she was growing deaf, and "McPherson" was worse. "It's the roaring of the creeks," she said. "Sometimes I think I'll go mad and I know I'm going deaf. I've stood there by the door on a spring morning when the snows are melting, and I've counted forty waterfalls, and the roar of them and the roar of the avalanches is enough to send a woman out of her mind! And then, it is lonely too—oh, you don't know what it is to see another face up here besides your children's! It's sometimes eighteen months, and once it was two full years, before I saw the face of living woman." '[3]

The river and the creeks gave constant promise of tragedy: ' "I had another little girl, and once when the floods were coming, down she ran after her father, and her foot slipped on the plank over the creek, and she was carried away. Her father's deaf and he never heard her cry; we found her when the creek went down." '[4] A relentless killer, the Matukituki did not finish with the McPhersons until 1919, when Mrs Duncan McPherson was drowned while returning from a rare visit to the world beyond the river.

In the autumn of 1920 a new family moved into the old homestead at the junction of the east and west branches. Jack Aspinall already knew the country, for he had worked at Cattle Flat Station before World War I. But his wife came from Liverpool, from the grimy environs of an industrial port to the arduous challenge of a back-country station. And the first years were hard. The original homestead burned down a few months after their arrival and two harsh winters in succession reduced the stock. This would have withered the spirit of less resilient people but the Aspinalls' buoyant determination countered the intransigent nature of their environment and Mount Aspiring Station became more than a hope and a name.

The Aspinalls became widely known for their hospitality; the growing population of mountaineers who moved into the Aspiring country had cause to remember them, not only for hospitality, but also for their help in mountain rescue and hut-building. Jack Aspinall took a keen interest in climbing activities and in 1929 took part in the fourth ascent of Mount Aspiring.

Climbing in the area began late compared to the Mount Cook region, but the object for any pioneering party was obvious—Aspiring, a glorious monolith of ice and snow standing apart from the Main Divide and guarded by glaciers and gorges. Its aloof stance on the western side of the Divide is its chief defence and the first approach from the west foundered through the difficulties of the Waiatoto River and the glaciers that ring the mountain's head.

[3]Maud Morland, *Through South Westland*, Christchurch, 1908. [4]ibid.

Bad weather at French Hut

In 1909 the opposite approach was tried and Major Bernard Head, with guides Jack Clarke of Mount Cook and Alex Graham of Franz Josef, travelled up the West Matukituki, enjoying the help and hospitality of Duncan McPherson. With professional skill and fine route-finding, a way was found up French Ridge and on to the Bonar Glacier beneath Aspiring's south face. On 23 November the ascent was completed.

More ascents followed, at wide intervals until the amateur climbing boom of the 1930s. Young climbers of that era turned to the myriad peaks that sequestered Aspiring, their imaginative names resounding in the mind—Stargazer, Skyscraper, Mainroyal, Fastness, Moonraker and Rob Roy. Huts were built, tracks cut, routes mapped out.

Since World War II the West Matukituki, and the East to a lesser extent, have become favourite haunts for climbers, trampers and hunters of all ages. Now it is possible to take four-wheel-drive vehicles to the palatial Aspiring Hut, once the limit of horses, and there is a high-altitude hut at the foot of Aspiring itself.

On a summer day, with a breeze ruffling the tussock, the river sparkling and murmuring, the sun's glare softened by the olive sweep of forest, the snow peaks friendly and shimmering, the Matukituki is a sum of warmth and ease, a place for indolent reflection. Yet, as in all mountain country, the warmth and ease derive from the disposition and character of the traveller, the nature of his ambitions, his strengths and failings. In mountains there is no room for weakness; they are inflexible when errors are made. . . .

In 1953 two climbers were lost in the ranges between the Matukituki and the Dart River to the west. Mountaineers went to search the ravine-riddled faces above Aspiring Hut and aircraft surveyed the open tops; one was an R.N.Z.A.F. Harvard carrying a well loved mountaineer, Christopher Johnson. Early on a clear and windless January morning the Harvard flew up the Matukituki to help in the search, passing over envious ground parties that were preparing for a hard climb through the forest: ' "That's the way to do it, no slogging up the hill." We all rather envied Christopher that morning which was so clean and fresh and held such bright promise.'[5] The plane flew over the main valley, then banked and climbed towards the western range and disappeared from sight.

A few hours later the ground parties were recalled to Aspiring Hut by rifle shots. The Harvard had crashed, unknown to everyone until its pilot had staggered shocked and bloodstained into the hut. With some difficulty the recalled men were able to ascertain where the plane had crashed, and they set out on a new search, spurred by the knowledge that a close friend lay injured and possibly dying in the wreckage.

'Beside the upturned fuselage and under the shelter of the torn-off wing, we found him, dead. He had a look of mild surprise in the blue eyes. Aubrey Bills had lifted him from the cockpit and laid him so that he could drink from a little stream of crystal water that ran twisting down the gully. Framed between the shiny rock walls, Aspiring soared to the sky, the train of the Bonar Glacier draped in haze-cream folds about the mountain's foot. A blackbird sang from the scrubline, and far away we heard the shrill call of a kea. It was a place of wonderful peace, and the feeling was so profound that for some time we didn't speak. We sat in the gully, silent, each busy with his own thoughts, and watched the hills.'[6]

[5]Paul Powell, *Men Aspiring*, Wellington, 1967. [6]ibid.

Physical hardship, the depths of the human spirit, beauty and tragedy span the century-old history of the Matukituki. Today modern transport and techniques make man's passage easier: generators provide electricity, the telephone line swings beside the river, an hour's drive will cover the distance between Wanaka and the two branches. Wanaka township has developed from a tiny settlement serving only farm and sawmill to a tourist and national-park centre attracting thousands of holidaymakers each summer. But the mountain lines are not redrawn, the big snows still fall to choke the valleys and crush the forest, the river floods and the boulders still groan beneath its waves.

The Aspinalls have closed a chapter in Matukituki history. Their new homestead is on the 'right' side of the river, beside the road. The old homestead, over the shingle and under the bluffs, is overgrown with fruit trees and flowering bushes, and is simply a reminder of the 1920s and before, when 'old McPherson' and his wife sat outside their rough dwelling and listened to the thunder of the river that governed life and death.

I closed the hut door, slamming out the wind and snow. Momentarily I was blind from the glare of white outside but as I dropped my pack on to the sleeping bench the recesses of the wood and iron came into focus. Our refuge from the storm was small: a single room about ten feet wide, twelve deep and eight high. There was a four-foot space between the door and the sleeping bench (eighteen inches high) which ran back to the western wall. Light was admitted by two windows, one about two feet by one beside the door, the other a tiny patch of glass near the roof at the back.

The French Ridge Hut is about twenty years old, though bits of it are older, dating from the original shelter which was collapsed by heavy snow. The rebuilt hut is sited on a more exposed position on the ridge so that wind can scour away dangerous drifts. I remembered this as a sudden, powerful gust hit the side of the hut and it seemed to lift slightly, shuddering.

Snow that had been blown through cracks in the door lay like a heap of salt on the frozen floorboards. The logbook confirmed that no one had been to the hut for a couple of months and there was a smell of dampness and decay. Mattresses doubled back for airing revealed damp stains and grime that we quickly covered with clothing and sleeping bags.

With a flash of flame and curses David lit the petrol stove. It spluttered into life and set up a dull roar, its head turning from dull grey to cherry red. The thought of food and hot drinks was warming in itself and drew a veil between the cold, indifferent world outside and our twelve-by-ten cocoon.

Like hedgehogs rolling up against danger, we withdrew from the hostile environment, even shrinking from the cold walls of the hut. Every action and thought was directed towards ease, warmth and security. Ambitions of climbing great peaks had dwindled until the greatest satisfaction was found in dry, clean socks that encouraged frozen toes to tingling warmth, or giant mugs of tea that burnt our lips and sent spasms of heat coursing through our bodies.

I lay in my sleeping bag, squinting in the poor light at the paperback which had proved to be the only intact book in the pile of yellow leaves on the shelf. With a concentration born of a complete lack of anything else to do, I followed the simple values of an unreal world of six guns and badmen, Silver Star saloons and heroic sheriffs. My alternative reading was a few loose pages of an ancient *Reader's Digest* which told me incompletely how to make a fortune on the stock exchange.

When the light became too dim for reading we rummaged in the litter of blackened billy lids, empty tins and packets of mildewed oats, and found candles to light and place in the window, as if we were providing a beacon for lonely travellers in the night. By candle-light the hut revealed softer lines; the damp patches on the wall-lining faded into the shadows, wet boots and unwashed pots were forgotten, beads of condensation glistened brightly on the metal.

We talked and talked of men and mountains, mountains and men, David puffing at an old pipe that smoked fitfully while I nurtured a slightly damp cigarette, meticulously tapping ash into a tin lid. Crumbling ash would have added little to the years-old grit and dirt that filled the wood seams, but social habits were set and there was comfort in order and discipline amid the chaos that reigned outside.

A candle blew out as a violent gust battered the hut. There was no thunder, but lightning suddenly flashed so brightly through the windows that the interior was filled with blue light, hurting our eyes. There was another flash, and another, so that we blew out the remaining candles and lay back, engaging in a game of counting flashes and timing the dense black pauses. The scene was unearthly as crackling splashes of light flooded into the tiny hut, accompanied only by the fluctuating bluster of wind and the rattle of drift against the walls. For the first time I was fully conscious of how thin our barricade was against the elements. As we counted more than a hundred flashes I slid deeper into my bag and moved slowly into sleep, the blue light penetrating even my closed eyelids.

I woke in a mood of hope and listened carefully to the temper of the wind. It had calmed and there was a quality to the daylight at the window that suggested sun and clear skies. The hut looked squalid; its attractions dissipated in the unflattering light of early morning. Now it only meant discomfort, hip bones aching from lying too long on a hard bed, lips sore from too-hot tea, hair matted, feet sweaty, bladder distended. The refuge was a prison and I longed for room to move and stretch.

With distaste I wrenched on frozen boots, tied ice-rimed laces and pulled open the door. The snow-reflected light was blinding but I smiled at the sight of broken cloud and patches of blue sky. Crunching awkwardly over the crusty snow, I walked to the edge of the ridge. Drift snow still hissed past my legs but the wind's force was spent. I could look down to the ice-encrusted terraces of Gloomy Gorge and further to the valley, a strip of green life breaking the miles of sterile white. Across the gorge Rob Roy looked like a wedding cake waiting to be cut, and down the ridge a party of keas shrieked crossly and flew in flashes of crimson. Taking a deep breath I shouted to David, so that he would come and see.



Bush waterfall,
West Matukituki

*Above* Winter on French Ridge

*Below* Summer on Wanaka beach

After the hunt,
Matukituki
Valley

Loading a wool bale

An old retainer

Trees and outbuildings, old Mount Aspiring homestead

New Year shearing muster

Jerry Aspinall of Mount Aspiring

Bunkhouse graffiti

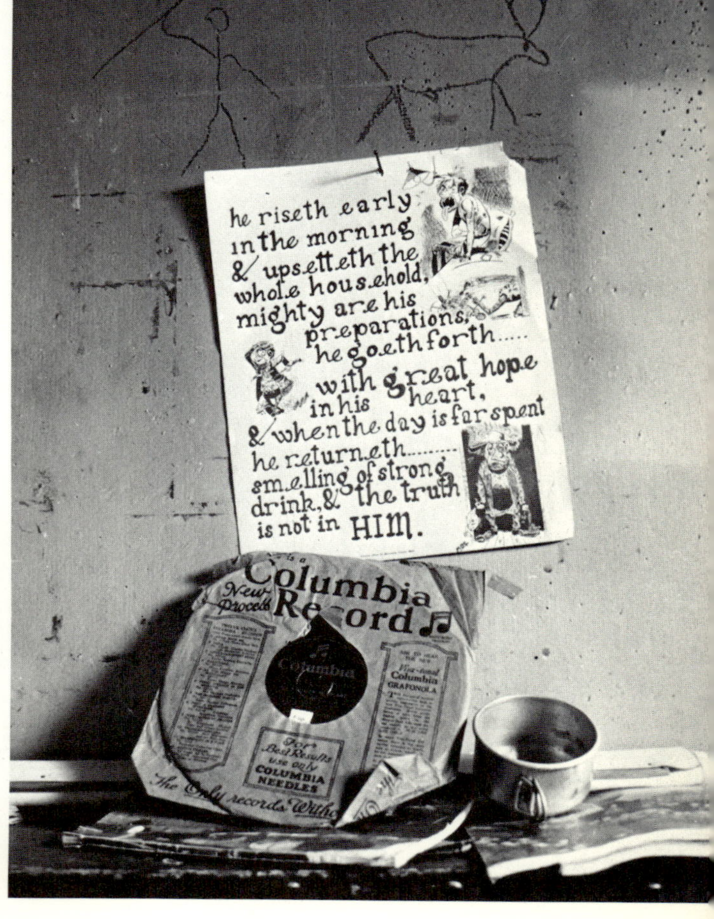

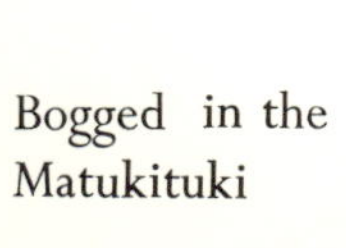

Bogged in the Matukituki

The West Matukituki Valley, with Cascade Hut on distant flat and Plunket Dome above

Mount
Aspiring

# THE BUSH AND THE RAIN

## *The Copland Valley*

Mountains nuzzle mountains
White-bearded rock-fronted
In perpetual drizzle.

Rivers swell and twist
Like a torturer's fist
Where the maidenhair
Falls of the waterfall
Sail through the air.

The mountains send below
Their cold tribute of snow
And the birch makes brown
The rivulets running down.

FROM 'Arawata Bill'
BY Denis Glover



*Overleaf* Looking up the Copland Valley at sunset

*Opposite*
Thermal spring near Welcome Flat Hut

Splinter Peak, Sierra Range

Bridge across the Copland River at Welcome Flat

# *The Bush and the Rain*

WITH a sense of triumph we climbed the last few feet of the ice face and stood upright. The view suddenly revealed was spectacular: from the summit of Mount Sefton we could look down its huge eastern face to the Hermitage Hotel, 8000 feet below, across the Hooker Valley to the ungainly bulk of Mount Cook, or north to the white walls of La Perouse. But most striking was the violent contrast between east and west. To the east lay hotel buildings, roads, yellow tussock, airstrips and shingly rivers. To the west, an icefield, range after range of rarely visited mountains, gorge after gorge of dense, unblemished forest; there was no mark of man and there seemed no possible way through the contorted hills that fell abruptly to the flat sheet of the Tasman Sea.

Colin and I sat on the summit for a few minutes, trying to contain and absorb a few parts of this great scene. It was difficult to find a mental perspective, for in a few hours we had been wrenched from one world to another. We had moved from a sultry morning at the Hermitage to the crisp and brilliant atmosphere of 10,000 feet, using a ski-plane in the first landings on the glacier to the west of Sefton. On the only fine day for weeks we had effortlessly climbed a great peak.

The weather would not hold for longer than this day. Far out over the Tasman a massive bank of cloud dominated the horizon; nearer, blobs of cotton-wool cloud formed over the forest and drifted in tight ranks towards the mountain. It was time to descend and seek the safety of the valley; but we were reassured by the thought of a returning ski-plane and a swift passage to comfort.

The descent of the ice face was easy, using the skilfully hewn steps of the incomparable guide, Harry Ayres, who had flown in before us with his client. With our bird's eye view we could pick out their figures, already well across the glacier towards the landing point. Lower down, ice changed to snow, wet and soft from the sun, and we ploughed on, sinking uncomfortably to our knees, sweating in the windless shelter of tottering ice towers that threatened to collapse in the heat.

At three o'clock we joined the others, seated on rocks from where they could look down to the Copland Valley. The cloud had thickened alarmingly and our underlying concern showed in our interpretation of every unusual sound as the distant hum of an aeroplane. I reflected on the meagre contents of my pack—spare clothes and chocolate—and watched as the bright green of the Copland was shadowed by the blossoming cloud.

This time it *was* an aeroplane and we jumped up quickly as it flashed behind the mountains, appearing and disappearing in the cloud that now began to hide the contours of ice and snow. We waited as the pilot circled, searching for a break that would give him a clear approach to the landing site. The minutes grew longer. Then all at once our fears were confirmed as the pilot waggled the plane's wings in a negative gesture, straightened out and disappeared for good over Sefton.

Harry accepted the plane's non-landing with equanimity. He had food and sleeping bags for his client and himself and was prepared for the worst, but I pondered uneasily on the

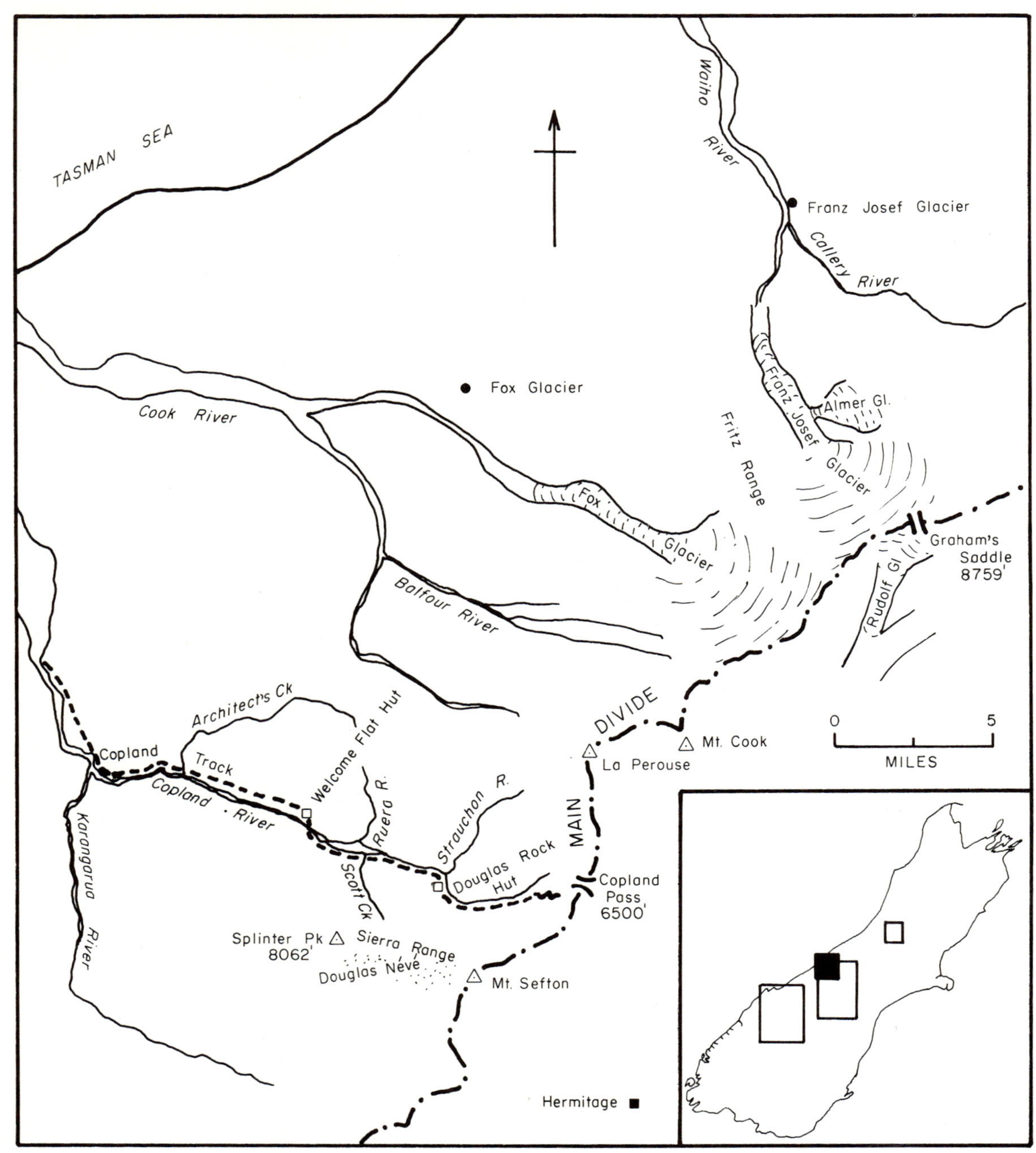


Spartan virtues of a cold bed and meagre supper. With an air of assurance and judgment derived from years of high climbing, he glanced at the small glacier that adorned the first slopes leading down to the distant Copland. The cloud was thicker now, obscuring the maze of lower gullies and bluffs; but Harry described in detail the route we must follow to reach the valley by nightfall. Then he sent Colin and me ahead to forge a trail in the snow, shouting directions from behind.

We became enveloped in thick fog. Crevasses loomed disconcertingly from the featureless swirl of white; occasional, intimidating glimpses of dripping rock walls above and below revealed the narrowness of our snowy bridge to safety. Harry's shouts grew more muffled and I glanced back frequently as his figure came and went, the fog so blurring my vision that I seemed to be looking through a badly focused lens.

Release came unexpectedly, as we kicked the snow from our boots, scrambled down a rocky spur and emerged beneath the base of the cloud. Here the first moss and tufts of gnarled tussock grew in crevices, and further down there were grassy basins and fingers of straggling bush. But no wide scree slope led to the valley floor, no tracked spur; the way was hedged by bluffs, dry watercourses and an unbroken mass of trees.

Harry led on, down, down, down, and our knees began to complain at the continuous steep descent. Rock, tussock, gravel, scrub, earth, speargrass, boulders and finally the bush, as we climbed, scrambled, jumped and slithered down the mountainside. It was a long summer day but the cloud shrouded the dwindling light; details of the landscape disappeared in the gloom and below there was just the dark mass of the bush and the faintly glimmering ribbon of the river.

Fingering an almost imperceptible blaze, Harry plunged into the bush and we followed, stumbling over unfamiliar roots, feeling our way in semi-darkness, nostrils filled with the smell of damp earth and rotting leaves. An old indistinct track led haphazardly down the steep slope and we slid over banks of crumbling earth, eager at the prospect of deliverance from the mountain.

Soon we heard the dull roar of a waterfall, a sound that broke into a day that had been full of barren silence. The roar grew louder and we stepped out of the bush to the increased lightness of glistening boulders and tumbling water, the fall cascading in one leap from high bluffs. Burying my face in the creek, I bathed my sunburnt face and swallowed mouthfuls of icy, bubbling water.

I stood up, gasping, and Harry waved down to where the creek met wide Welcome Flat and the pale outline of the Copland track. He described the way and sent me ahead to find the hut, light a fire and set the billy boiling.

The grassy flat was luxury to my tired eyes but it was strangely awkward to walk an even path again. A wave of fatigue overtook me and I slumped to the ground, resting my pack against a fallen tree. Stretched out, I longed for a sleeping bag so that I could sleep where I lay, staring up at the drifting strands of now-harmless cloud and the scatter of stars that began to appear in the darkening sky.

After a while a gentle tugging at my pack roused me. Absentmindedly I shifted position but the tugging continued. Half afraid, I looked around. Unabashed, two keas hopped on to the log behind me and leant forward, cocking their heads in great suspicion. They made no sound and did not move as I stood up and stared back at them, loudly casting doubts on their parentage. As if stupefied, they sat motionless and watched as I picked up my axe and walked on.

At the far end of the flat I paused as four deer emerged from the edge of the forest, noted my unfamiliar figure with a mixture of mild curiosity and disdain and ambled back into the trees. Beyond them in the half darkness I saw the overgrown bridge spanning the river and the sharp line of the hut roof. A whiff of sulphur from hot springs drifted over the water. Stooping, I began collecting dry branches for the fire.

⟡

The Copland is the main tributary of the Karangarua River, joining it a few miles east of the suspension bridge carrying the highway south to the Haast Pass and Otago. On the north side of the bridge a yellow pointer sign reads 'Copland Pass', inviting travellers to undertake a twenty-five-mile tramp to the Copland headwaters and the high alpine pass giving direct access to the Hooker Glacier and Mount Cook. In the 1890s it was hoped that this route could be transformed into a highway, linking Fox and Franz Josef to the Hermitage, saving tourists the long, backtracking journey via Arthur's Pass. Today there is still talk of a road and the driving of a tunnel through the mountains.

But in the first days of European settlement in New Zealand the West Coast was thought to be of no use to tourists or anyone else. Cook wrote in 1770: 'No country upon earth can appear with a more ruged and barren aspect . . .'

An impression of the South Island, formed from sealers' familiarity with its western coasts, caused Jules de Blosseville to write in 1823: 'If some day these lands are colonised by Europeans the South Island will only be a branch of the north . . .'[1]

The explorations of Thomas Brunner and Charles Heaphy in 1846-47 and of Leonard Harper in 1857 did nothing to enhance the prospect of settlement in the region and only tantalising rumours of gold spurred explorers and prospectors. It is daunting country, a hyperbole of nature without gentle plains for human commerce; broken, glaciated mountains and bluff-ridden foothills fall into a tangle of forest, denying space for agriculture. So precipitous is the land between the Main Divide and the harsh Tasman Sea that rivers have no room for meanders and descend in torrent and shingle bed to a harbourless coast. The Christchurch *Press* once compared the two sides of the Canterbury Province of the 1850s: on the west, 'gloomy skies, incessant rain, a country wrapped in perpetual solitude, incapable of occupation, niggardly of promise'; on the east, 'fine weather, a country easily crossed in all directions, a land ready to welcome an industrious population to its breast'.[2]

The country was hostile to human industry but overflowed with magnificent scenery, though a member of Julius von Haast's survey party in 1860 experienced a surfeit: 'I am getting sick of fine scenery and mountains and longing for open country.'[3] And scenery would not bring development to the Coast, only gold.

In 1864 the presence of payable gold was confirmed at last; the West Coast skies grew brighter, the rain eased, its solitude was broken and its promise was grand. The Arthur's Pass road from Christchurch was quickly cut, towns sprang up and by 1866 there were 103 pubs in Hokitika.

In the wake of the gold rush von Haast in 1865 took a geological survey party south of the main diggings. From Okarito he saw the Franz Josef Glacier, plunging from its huge alpine snowfields through the foothills and into the forest . . . 'Forming with its pure unsullied

[1] P. R. May, *The West Coast Gold Rushes*, Christchurch, 1962. [2] ibid. [3] ibid.

ice, broke in numberless seracs, a most remarkable and striking contrast to the surrounding landscape.'[4]

Neither the Franz Josef nor the Fox Glacier had been visited before. Brunner in 1847 had forded the Waiho and Cook rivers but their milky waters had not caused him to reflect on their glacial origins, nor to discover the tongues of clear, tortured ice that descended to within 700 feet and ten miles of the sea. In 1859 two men who had searched for grazing land from the sea described one of the glaciers for the first time; but Haast and his party were the first to examine both at close quarters. They were entranced by the beauty of 'unsullied' ice surrounded by pines, ratas, beeches and 'arborescent ferns'. Von Haast wrote: 'One of my European companions could only compare [it] to the magnificent scenery of some London Christmas pantomime.'[5]

A few months after von Haast's visit to the Franz Josef, prospectors probed the Waiho for gold until 'stopped by a large glacier'.[6] Yet the Waiho and its tributaries, notably the Callery, gave worthwhile yields until the turn of the century. Prospectors went further south and in 1867 a twenty-seven-year-old Scottish migrant lately from the Otago goldfields—Charles Edward Douglas—fossicked for gold up the Karangarua and Copland as far as Architect's Creek. It is likely that other diggers wandered up the Copland before him but to this man, better known as 'Mr Explorer Douglas', we owe the first full exploration of the Copland watershed and, indeed, of most of the southern West Coast valleys.

Douglas's career of exploration began in 1868. For the next twenty years he pioneered the gorges and the river beds from the Cascade in the south to the Balfour in the north, sometimes working for the Survey Department, sometimes at odd jobs that could never hold him for long. In 1889 he began full-time work for the department and three years later went up the Copland to determine if there was a pass at its head suitable for a road to the Hermitage.

Today one can walk from the Karangarua bridge to the foot of the Copland Pass in about ten hours. The track is clear, broad enough for a horse in its lower reaches, bridged at the worst river and creek crossings, and the journey can be broken at two sturdy huts—Welcome Flat in the middle valley and Douglas Rock near the bushline. But for Douglas in 1892, 'The Copeland is the only River in Westland that I have been forced to clear my way with Bill hook.'[7]

Though the journey of exploration was wearisome for a man past the physical prime of life, there were some compensations. There were views of cataracts and the river strewn with boulders worn to fantastic shapes and others so large they supported fully grown rata trees. There was the delight of breaking from the bush on to Welcome Flat, twelve miles up valley: '[flats] are a Godsend to travellers, the delight of breaking out on one of them after miles of scrambling in dense bush more than repays all the trouble, and then the scenery can be appreciated. Occasional glimpses of Peaks and Glaciers through dense foliage may be very pretty and verry Artistic but they are aggravating to ordinary mortals.'

Of the scenery Douglas saw from Welcome Flat, he was especially impressed by the range

[4]J. von Haast, *Geology of the Provinces of Canterbury and Westland*, Christchurch, 1879. [5]ibid. [6]May, op. cit.
[7]John Pascoe (ed.), *Mr Explorer Douglas*, Wellington, 1957. The Douglas quotations which follow are from the same source.

on the south he named Sierra, 'one of the wonders of the Copeland'. He saw it as a range 'of broken shattered cliffs, topped by a serrated ridge looking as if some Giant with little skill and a very bad file had attempted to make a saw out of the Mountains'.

The scenery was fit to delight the eye of any tourist and the birdlife was prolific: 'The Weka prowled around the Tent, anexing anything portable and the Kiwi made night hedious with its piercing shriek. The Blue Duck crossed over to whistle a welcome. The Caw Caw swore and the Kea skirled. . . .' But he expressed fear at the birds' fate from the wild progeny of diggers' dogs, cats, rats and ferrets. When Arthur Harper walked down the Copland three years after Douglas, these introduced animals had already taken a heavy toll. Today the silence of Welcome Flat is oppressive and there are few signs of birds on the river and its terraces. The forest is more heartening, with curious tomtits and bellbirds, tame pigeons and furtive wekas stalking deliberately behind the ineffective camouflage of low ferns.

Douglas discovered that the head of the Copland and its upper tributary, the Strauchon, were not suitable for a road pass. He saw a likely pass for adventurous travellers on foot—probably the future Copland Pass. It was free of snow but the time was early autumn and he felt sure that winter snows and avalanches would preclude its use by horse traffic.

That was not the end of the story. Arthur Harper (son of Leonard Harper, the explorer), following the instructions of the Survey Department, crossed the Copland Pass in 1895 from the Hermitage and proved it a worth-while route. A few weeks earlier the English climber E. A. Fitzgerald with his guide Mattias Zurbriggen had also crossed the range and gone down the Copland in more arduous fashion. It was clear that the Copland did offer the most direct and reasonable route from the West Coast glaciers to the Mount Cook region. Following these crossings, Douglas's final recommendations in 1895 were fulfilled almost to the letter: a foot track, benched where necessary, bridged across Architect's Creek, cairns to guide people over the pass itself and 'an iron hut either at the foot of the saddle or on Welcome Flat' (both were built). Later, Douglas and two other men blazed a track up the Copland and his mates discovered the hot mineral springs at the western end of Welcome Flat.

Subsequently the Copland track and its facilities were developed until it became a popular excursion for tourists under the aegis of guides. After World War II its popularity waned, coincident with the decline of guiding, the increase in amateur climbing and the 'new look' in tourism—package coach tours that took in half the South Island at speed and precluded the deeper, if more arduous, delights of a transalpine crossing and a journey through the uninhibited abundance and grandeur of a West Coast valley. By the end of the 1950s the Copland track was overgrown, barred by windfalls. The Architect's Creek bridge provided a more dangerous crossing than the ford and the Welcome Flat Hut was without bunks and a windowless haven for sandflies. Reprieve came in 1960 when the Westland National Park was formed, and a decade later the track had recovered to the state of earlier days. Now dozens of enterprising trampers use the pass each summer, indulging in the acres of natural subalpine gardens at the head of the valley and easing tired limbs in the hot pools at Welcome Flat.

The Copland Pass and track make up one-half of a round trip through the high mountains

Architect's Creek during and after a flood

which, for diversity of scenery within a comparatively short distance, is unequalled in the Southern Alps. The other half involves a traverse of the Franz Josef Glacier to Graham's Saddle at its head, then down the Rudolf, a tributary of the Tasman Glacier, and on to the Hermitage. Graham's Saddle was first proved by Arthur Harper in 1895 when he took Fitzgerald and Zurbriggen across; he then went on to return to the West Coast through his first crossing of the Copland Pass. He was the first to make a round trip that ranges in height from near sea level to almost 9000 feet, encompassing icefall and forest, snowfield and tussock flat, glacier and river.

Douglas and Harper, singly or together, pioneered all the country between the Franz Josef and the Karangarua in the 1890s. Douglas was old enough to be Harper's father but the two worked well together and Harper learnt much from Douglas's vast experience of the West Coast bush. Something of this, and of Douglas's quaint sense of humour, can be discovered in a little of his bush philosophy, which Harper was fond of recalling in later years. On fording flooded rivers: 'Not being able to swim has saved my life many a time.' On the flavour of kiwi in a stew: 'Like an old bit of pork boiled in a second-hand coffin.' On the value of barometers: 'I wouldn't worry about the barometer, if I were you, it doesn't affect the weather much on the Coast.'[8]

Douglas's great but self-effacing contribution to the understanding of South Westland was well appreciated by the department he worked for and by his few intimates such as Harper, but otherwise his ability and work went largely unnoticed. No seeker of fame, he scorned those who worked for honours or claimed the merit for other people's discoveries. He engraved a more enduring memorial with his painstaking survey work and his dogged, sustained efforts to fulfil his instructed or self-imposed exploratory briefs. As John Pascoe wrote: 'South Westland can count him son by migration, sweat, hazard, exploration, and by mortal loneliness and bitter end. Consider Douglas as an imperishable part of our frontier tradition.'[9]

The Fox and Franz Josef glaciers became the focal tourist attractions of the West Coast and increasing numbers came to visit the region as railway, road and hotels were built and improved. Franz Josef became the more important centre, perhaps because it was more accessible, but the Graham family developed strong guiding traditions there and a reputation for hospitality. Alex Graham is a legendary name in Westland mountaineering and, with his two most well known companions, the Rev. H. E. Newton and Dr E. Teichelmann, he made first ascents of six of the great 10,000-foot peaks. His brother Peter created a similar record and reputation when he was chief guide at the Hermitage between 1908 and 1922.

The Grahams' Glacier Hotel, Waiho, was built in 1908. Before that, accommodation for visitors was provided in 'a punga house, i.e. built of fern-logs on end, filled in with moss and grass. A house of this kind may even grow. . . . '[10] There was also a store and post office and a weekly coach service. After World War I travel conditions improved with the completion of the railway from Christchurch to Hokitika and Ross, and with regular connecting motor services along a road that was little more than a rough track.

[8]A. P. Harper, *Memories of Mountains and Men.* [9]*Mr Explorer Douglas*, p. viii.
[10]Maud Morland, *Through South Westland.*

The original Glacier Hotel burned down in 1954 and the area languished until the tourist boom of the 1960s. The road south over the Haast Pass, joining the Coast to the southern lakes district of Otago, was opened at the end of 1965, creating a new tourist circuit whereby travellers could circumnavigate the Southern Alps by car. A new Government hotel was opened at Franz Josef to cater for burgeoning trade. The planes of Mount Cook Air Services supplemented road traffic with a regular ferry service from the Hermitage, and it became possible to fly from Franz Josef or Fox to Sydney within half a day. The road journey from the Karangarua bridge to Hokitika, which now takes three hours, took Arthur Harper four days on horseback in 1895.

Improved communications are a boon not only to tourists but also to mountaineers and other transient inhabitants of the West Coast back country, who can reach the scene of their explorations with greater ease. But one shies at the thought of a rolling tourist boom bulldozing more forest for strips of asphalt, felling rata trees for overhead wires. Perhaps much of the West Coast high country will remain intact within the boundaries of the Westland National Park; but economic expediency can bend conservation laws and tourist facilities can become as valuable as scenery.

The uncompromising nature of the land may be its final safeguard—and the determined wish of many to discover the country in its natural state, to find in unspoiled mountains the refreshment of spirit that is increasingly denied by the aspirations and demands of modern society. With apologies to Charlie Douglas, though 'aggravating to ordinary mortals . . . occasional glimpses of Peaks and Glaciers through dense foliage may be very pretty and very Artistic'.

With dull acceptance I shouldered my pack and plunged into the first ford. The wind came in violent gusts off the sea, roaring up the Karangarua so that the leaves of the cabbage trees clattered in frenzy and the rows of fern trees bent in submission. The rain claimed the whole day and in the direction of the upper Karangarua and the Copland nothing could be seen but forbidding, blackly-forested hillsides rising into a low scud of grey cloud. I walked as fast as heavy pack and squelching boots would allow, anxious to leave the first tussock flats for the forest as sheets of rain swept up the valley and lashed at my back.

The forest gave me a sense of security. The steady drips, the dribbling streams that commandeered the broad track, the occasional groan of old limbs as the wind gusted in the treetops—all transmitted a feeling of permanence, of a pattern of life that was not easily changed by the bluster of storms. The birds were sheltering from the rain but sometimes a bedraggled tomtit emerged silently and suddenly from the mute forest to watch me pass. And once there was a flurry of shadows as deer dashed fluidly to safety up the hillside.

Except for these timid showings of animal life I was alone; and my initial feeling of security became tinged with anxiety as small streams began to tumble more aggressively across the track and the Copland River's distant roar grew louder. My clothing and pack were soaked, a damp cold penetrated the sweaty warmth beneath my parka and I soon eyed each overhanging boulder with thoughts of shelter from the rushing water and brooding trees. The man-made track, and the promise of the hut at its end, were my only solace and spur.

On the open river bed the rain and storm were displayed in their full power. The river coursed down its narrow valley in gigantic waves and the boulders at its edge became submerged as its level rose in the few minutes that I stood and watched in awe. High above on the bluffs, waterfalls blossomed like flowers in the desert after rain, enjoying brief hours of life and spectacle.

Further on I came to Architect's Creek, which thundered through the forest, bank to bank, grey and terrifying. I did not appreciate the full extent and violence of the flood until I returned three days later. Then the creek meandered gently in three white streams through a wilderness of boulders.

With care I moved across the one-man suspension bridge, distracted by the footway's slight cant, vividly aware of what one false step would mean. Frequently I had to wrench my eyes away from the heaving mass of water below to concentrate on the next step. Then the bridge began to rise again and with relief I reached the suspension tower.

Dropping into the forest, I was anxious now about the three remaining creeks that lay between Architect's and Welcome Flat Hut. They were unbridged and in flood could be dangerous for a man alone. It was not long before my anxiety was confirmed and I faced a cascade which at first sight seemed impassable. Despairingly I thought of waiting until the flood subsided, but it was late and this would mean a miserable bivouac in the bush. The desire for a dry bed and warm meal overcame fear.

I studied the rapids, the pools, the rocks submerged or standing dry, calculated the force of water and the consequences of a slip, then, using my ice axe for support, edged into the freezing, turbulent current, the water rising over my thighs, pushing and snatching as I lifted my boots to feel for secure footholds. Long, long minutes passed as I manœuvred across, balancing against the current until I was able to stretch for a boulder on the opposite bank and haul myself to safety.

The worst was over. The rain stopped and the noise of rushing water was broken by the songs of rejuvenated birds. A pigeon, tumbling and soaring in the torn skeins of mist, portrayed release from a baneful day. A gap in the foliage was framed by flaming rata blossoms and, as the running water receded on the track, a petrified stream of fallen red needles lined the scoured earth. On the ridge tops dense cloud gave way to fragments of blue sky and the sickly yellow light of the late sun briefly illuminated the drenched leaves.

The forest thinned and, as the trees parted, I saw with delight the steam from hot pools lifting to join the mist. Incongruous in the wild landscape, the roof of the hut appeared, embodying refuge and warmth, food and perhaps company. I had come to Welcome Flat hut before at dusk, down from Sefton. Then, as now, it promised all that I could wish for.



*Opposite* La Perouse
from the Cook River

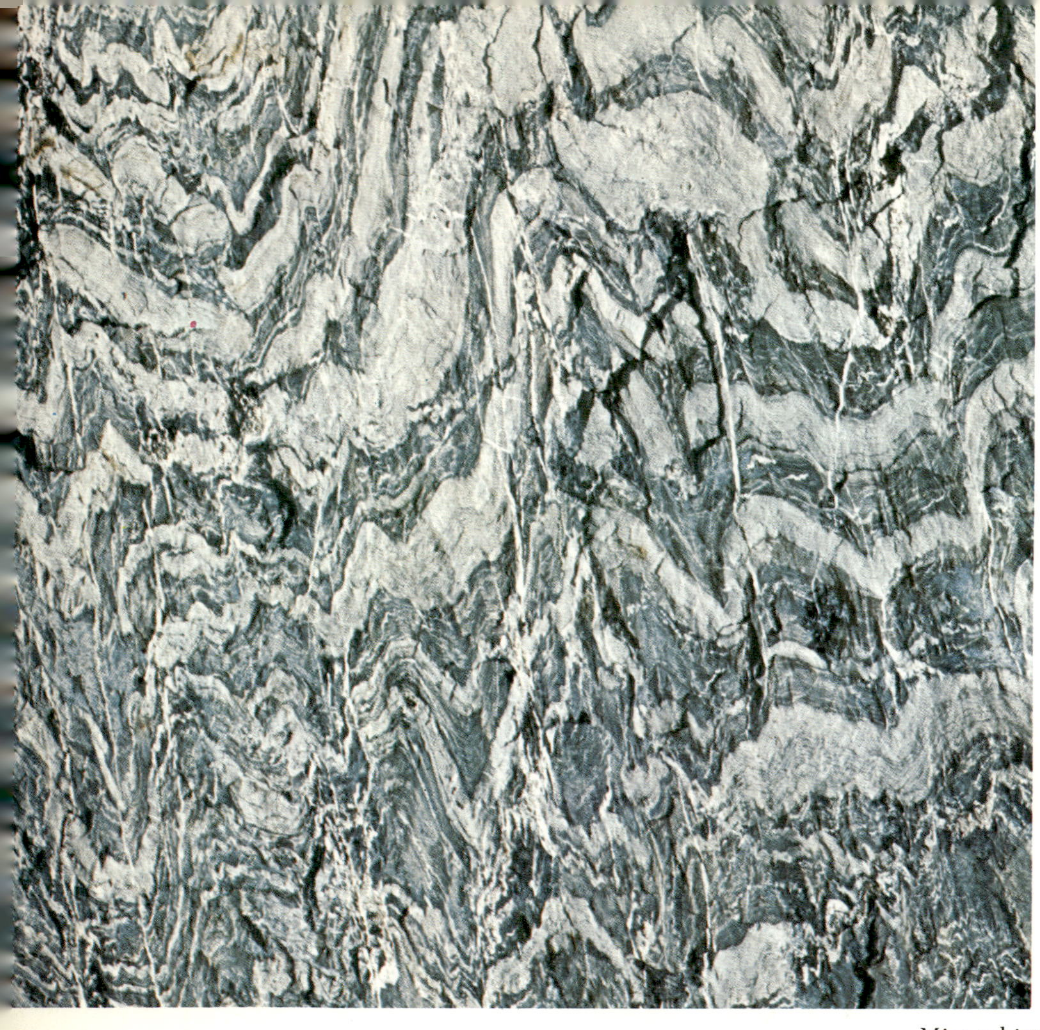

Mica schist

*Celmisia hectori*

Greywacke with brown weathering crust and some lichen

An alga, *Trentepohlia* sp.

New Zealand edelweiss, *Leucogenes grandiceps*

Buttercup, *Ranunculus* sp.

Gentian, *Gentiana* sp.

Large mountain daisy, *Celmisia coriacea*

Old man's beard lichen, *Usnea* sp.

Mountain foxglove, *Ourisia* sp.

Mount Cook lily, *Ranunculus lyallii*

*Above* Talus

*Below* Mountain pool

Mountain totara above Franz Josef Glacier

Boulders in the Copland Valley

Looking down the Fox Glacier at sunset

# MOUNTAIN ENCOUNTER

The mountains crouch like tigers—or await
As women wait. The mountains have no age.
But O the heart leaps to behold them loom:
A sense as of vast fate rings in the blood; no refuge,
No refuge is there from the flame that reaches

Among familiar things and makes them seem
Trivial, vain.

FROM 'The Mountains'
BY James K. Baxter



*Overleaf* Climbing into the sun, Glacier Dome

Party on the face of the Minarets, with Tasman Glacier below and Malte Brun across the valley

Ice climber

*Below* The ranges in winter: looking across and down Jagged Stream to the Rakaia River, Arrowsmith Range

# Mountain Encounter

AT DAWN we scrambled down moraine heaps to the first patch of dirty, old ice. The mountain lay before us, too close for us to unravel the secrets of its design: it was silhouetted against the pale pink and blue sky, a magnificent ruin with pinnacled ridges climbing to the summit like weathered flying buttresses. The western rock face was blank and uninviting; ice flowed greyly from its lower margin, rippling and gaping across the basin, ending in pulverised lumps down the side of bluffs. The rock ridge we had come to climb edged the glacier circumspectly, met with the western face, then rolled on broadly to the curved cornices of the distant summit. My stomach tightened as I tried to assess the difficulty and nature of each pinnacle and rent. One never knew what lay in wait.

With growing daylight, the last dregs of early morning lethargy disappeared and I felt a surge of enthusiasm as Peter handed me the end of the rope. Peter, fair, stocky and cheerful, alleviating moments of self-doubt, unwinding tension with a joke. A few yards away Graham and John sat on boulders, purposefully strapping on crampons. Before us lay a steep slope of hard snow, rising a thousand feet to the upper glacier and then the ridge. Graham, nondescript in worn breeches and patched tartan shirt, brought method and calm assurance to an enterprise. He said little, in contrast to John who, with dark, sparkling eyes, exclaimed at every new facet of the mountain world that caught his fancy. John had never climbed high before; but his evident strength and eagerness would be enough, I reasoned, aided by the combined talents of the rest. As we started up the snow, he followed Graham like a veteran.

It was a familiar rhythm: in with the axe, one, two steps, axe, one two, boot and crampon kicked cleanly into the crisp, compacted snow. I bent to the task, enjoying the growing warmth in my limbs, watching with satisfaction as the valley receded beneath my feet. Axe *in*, one two kicks, sucking in the still, frozen air; axe *in*, one two, glancing between my legs to see that my speed suited Peter's rhythm, that the rope did not drag in the snow.

As we gained height, I looked up more and more, seeking to understand the rock and ice that lay ahead. A breeze fluttered past, chilling my arms; a spindrift of snow scurried over the slope; and a ray of yellow light suddenly washed a rib of rock high on the western face, growing quickly in intensity. The mountain was coming to life.

At the top of the snow slope we traversed more slowly on to the humps and treacherous hollows of the glacier. A sense of danger came for the first time as we probed with our axes for the secret trapdoors of crevasses; here the shaft came roughly against hard ice, there it sank into soft snow with disconcerting ease, leaving a puncture, a black circle in the soft whiteness, marking the frozen, slippery pit that lay beneath our feet. With care we backed away, adjusting ropes, taking a new course, moving towards the solid rock of the ridge that loomed larger over our heads.

Confidence grew, we climbed with increased speed, chopped steps up a steep bank and emerged on to a shelf which rippled easily to a saddle on our ridge. A new world was



Rock
climber

revealed. We could see 3000 feet down to the great valley glacier that swept between ranks of innumerable peaks. The sky was filled with mountains.

Beyond the saddle all was bathed in brilliant sunlight, the reflection off miles of snow and ice daunting to the eye. Behind us, the valley, snow slope and glacier lay silent in a grey and black half-world of cold shadow. Looking up the broken ridge, I watched with pleasure as the sharp line of sunlight crept down the rock towards us. The tip of the peak was just visible over the humps and blocks, etched into the purely blue sky. Suddenly Peter yodelled and involuntarily I repeated his call as the welling of joy and happiness within me demanded release. With new energy and enthusiasm, I kicked the snow from my boots and grasped the rough rock, reaching up towards the sun.

Balancing, pressing, jamming, pulling and stretching, we insinuated our way along the intricacies of the ridge. Instinctively we climbed in the sun, shying away from crevices decorated grotesquely with slowly dripping icicles. The face beneath our feet, sweeping down from the ridge top, paused momentarily in its fall then dropped in one unbroken wall to a crumpled icefall that twisted wickedly to the wide highway of the main valley glacier.

Seeking cracks for our fingers, ledges for our boots, we moved steadily upwards, following the rise and fall of the rock. Sometimes we paused to remove loose stones that threatened safety or to flick the rope over jagged spikes. Warming to the sun, I was filled with a sense of well-being that only physical freedom and confidence could generate. I revelled in the challenge the mountain offered, found delight in the patterns of brown and black rock, the delicate curls of pristine snow, the little blankets of furry lichen that softened the austerity of a high landscape that was cracked and splintered by wind and frost.

Higher up, Peter and I stopped to let the others lead. I leaned back, soaking up the warmth, commenting rudely on the ragged seat of Graham's trousers as he moved past. John appeared, scrambling over the rock with difficulty as if he were trying to keep contact with all four limbs at once. His eager look had changed to one of grim determination; he moved by without comment, panting slightly. I looked at Peter and read in his expression a confirmation of what I feared. My carefree air faded, as if black clouds had suddenly rolled over the ranges to the west.

I grasped the rough rock to begin climbing again and remembered the first time I had climbed up a snow slope and stepped on to a high ridge. The ground had lost all solidity and, as if I were standing on the crest of a cathedral roof, one false step had seemed to invite disaster. I could understand John's mental predicament; his confidence had disappeared at the sight of the space beneath his feet. I looked down involuntarily and the ridge seemed to sway slightly. The glittering summit was further away.

I followed John closely, assessing his plight, as Graham came to an awkward twenty-foot step in the ridge. It was complicated by loose blocks, but with great finesse he gently climbed this treacherous pitch and anchored the rope above for John's safety. John was undecided and diffident. We urged him on, passing advice as he dragged himself clumsily from hold to hold. Near the top of the step he came to an ugly, bulging block that rocked dangerously as he edged upwards. Instinctively, I knew what would happen.

Swinging round, I scrambled back down the ridge, then stopped as a horrible grating sound broke the balance of blue sky and warm rock.

John's feet kicked wildly for support as the block came away and fell with a crash that seemed to shake the whole ridge. There was a shower of sparks before it disappeared in a dozen pieces down the face; and the rumble of falling rock was broken only by a pathetic half sob, half shriek, as John dangled like a gaping fish from Graham's tight rope. A reek laced the air as if a big gun had been fired.

Swiftly Peter and I climbed up and balanced beside him, grasping his arms and helping him until he reached the safety of Graham's anchor. He flopped down, shaking and dejected, head between his hands, staring at the rock between his boots. A few terse words of comfort and inquiry were enough. John could not go on, and he would not go back down the ridge; he could face the cathedral roof no longer. In a few minutes the mood had changed from one of confidence and success to uncertainty and danger.

With a mixture of despair, annoyance and foreboding, I looked up at the silent glistening summit and the clear sky. It was midday; by three we would have been on top. Abruptly I turned away and looked down at the complex of gullies and ribs that formed the face above the glacier we had left that morning. I could pick out our tracks in the snow, meandering from the top of the now-distant snow slope towards the saddle, a thousand feet down the ridge. Instinct told me that we should return the way we had come—better the devil we knew. But John's state precluded that. Returning down the ridge might invite total collapse.

The weight of decision was heavy. The others seemed to hang on my judgment now that leadership was more than nominal. A short distance up the ridge there was another saddle. From it a steep, unbroken snow gully swooped invitingly down to the glacier. At the bottom the glacier ice broke away sharply from the face, leaving a gap in the form of a huge crevasse. From where we stood it was impossible to tell the width of the crevasse. Its upper lip overhung, hiding either an uncrossable chasm or the tenuous path to safety of a snow bridge. The crevasses on the glacier beyond offered little comfort, for the ice looked as if it had been ruptured by an earthquake. But there was no other way down.

Once we were committed to the gully, the difficulties of our situation were magnified. Enthusiasm and enjoyment waned rapidly as we left the sun of the ridge for the cold shade. The gully was steeper than I had expected, its icy snow harder, and it took three jarring kicks to form a safe step. I watched anxiously as John moved tentatively down the line of the steps, searching carefully for each hole with the toe of his boot, like a fly lethargic from cold shifting uncertainly down a white wall.

Graham shepherded John while Peter and I took turns to kick steps. I felt keenly the responsibility of finding a way to safety, but Graham shouldered perhaps a greater burden. John had to be coddled and eased down the mountain; he had to be encouraged and safeguarded and made to believe that our retreat was nothing out of the ordinary, that return to the glacier, the valley and the hut was just a matter of time. And Graham had to descend last, knowing that he could not rely on John's ropework to save him if he fell. He must not fall, nor show any sign of faltering, both for his own safety and for the sake of John's thin thread of confidence. It would have been easier to climb alone.

The constant kicking was hard work. Toes felt bruised and flashes of pain began to shoot up my shins. My knees began to shake with the effort and more frequently I found excuses to pause—so that I could gauge progress, check the time or decide on the direction of the next row of steps. Thankfully I would reach the limit of the rope, stop, cut out a platform then ram in my axe to safeguard Peter while he climbed down. Awkwardly he would pass my stance and launch laboriously on the next fifty steps. Paradoxically, I became impatient for him to finish as I eked the rope out inch by inch. As I waited, my feet slowly froze, my fingers fared little better in ice-encrusted mitts, and showers of loose snow, dislodged by Graham and John above, hissed down the slope on to my head and down my neck. Cramped and stiff with cold, I envied Peter his work yet knew that soon after I resumed step-kicking I would like nothing better than to stop.

Hours passed and our rate of progress slowed as a dispirited tiredness overtook us. Our descent was an unsatisfactory course of necessity, not spurred by the stimulus of success. Alarmed, I looked out over the unfriendly mountains and saw the valleys gathering gloom. My watch confirmed that only an hour remained before darkness.

Once again I reached the rope's limit and stopped kicking. I looked down and saw with relief that the upper lip of the big crevasse lay only fifty feet away. As I waited for Peter to come down, I knew that the findings of the next few minutes would determine the nature of our beds that night. Impatient to dispel the uncertainty, I began climbing down before Peter had secured his axe. Urgency lent power to my boots and soon I could scrape the lip of the crevasse with the blade of my axe. While Peter kept the rope tight, I stood upright and leaned slightly forward, peering over the edge.

Awed and sickened, I drew back. There was nothing but the blue-black hole of the crevasse, thirty feet wide, its nether lip fifty feet lower. There was no bridge. To the right the crevasse narrowed to meet a brow of overhanging rock on the side of the gully. To the left the prospect was less final—a tumble of rock and contorted, bare ice through which we might fashion a route. It was Hobson's choice.

I became aware that movement above me had ceased and looked up to see three blank, waiting faces. I shook my head and gestured unconvincingly to the left. I started kicking steps again and my feeling of despair gave way to resignation and then, suddenly, to a mood of light-hearted humour. It was all so ridiculous. I could picture acquaintances, at that very moment, putting away gardening tools and wiping the day's sweat from their brows as they uncorked a flagon of beer and looked forward to a hot meal, a good programme on television and a comfortable bed. Here, four cold hungry mountaineers were stranded in the snow with no better prospect for a night's comfort than a flask of water, a bar of choco-

Berg-
schrund

late and a bed of ropes. The moon shone brightly with the glow of the setting sun, anchored to a pinnacle on the ridge. It would freeze hard, too.

In a spirit of comradeship and shared misfortune we gathered beneath the rock on the left side of the gully. John was quiet and pensive but Graham punctuated our discussion by tossing small stones into the crevasse, accompanied by frightful oaths, and Peter described the decor of our magnificent bedroom with pungent wit. For there was no hope of crossing the big crevasse, and the others lower down the glacier, before darkness fell. During the little daylight that remained we had to make our bed where we were and lie on it.

A corrugation in the ice above the crevasse offered some protection from the vindictive breeze that had sprung up. There was a small flat area within it, peppered with small rock fragments that had fallen from the face above. We untied the ropes and spread them over these and then, to our delight, Graham produced a groundsheet to make our comfort complete. Pulling on every stitch of clothing, we huddled together, boots off, feet rammed into our packs, and settled down to a daunting twelve-hour vigil.

No bedroom view was more impressive. A final creamy light illuminated the high peaks to the south as the glaciers beneath shrank into the purple and black vaults of the valleys. More and more stars bloomed in the darkening sky, sharp and brilliant, dimmed only by a searchlight moon that shifted behind the ridges, casting grotesque shadows across the silvered snow of the glacier. Near at hand snow crystals glittered with dazzling reflection and the entire landscape was so smoothed and calmed by silence and light that its latent hostility was lost. The occasional rattle of falling stones had ceased with the deepening frost, the drip of a melting icicle had stopped, and the only movement and sound outside our tiny human conclave was the scurry and whisper of a capricious breeze.

Cigarettes helped to pass the time and provided a focus of pleasure. Their red glow suggested warmth, their smoke relaxed stiff and tired limbs and staved off hunger. We had not eaten for half a day but agreed not to prepare our meagre supper until nine or ten o'clock in an attempt to break the night's monotony. At this time, Graham gathered the scraps of food in our packs and solemnly announced the contents of our meal: a bar of chocolate and half a tube of condensed milk. With ingenuity he built a cradle of stones for a few pieces of solid fuel secreted in the first-aid pouch. He lit these to heat a pannikin in which he melted snow, chocolate and milk. It was the finest drink I had ever tasted.

I woke suddenly and realised, to my surprise, that I had slept. My right side felt like a block of wood and when I shifted I was gripped by painful spasms of cramp. My whole body was chilled. The breeze returned and flicked over my shoulders, causing me to break into uncontrollable shivering. John began shivering too, then Peter, then Graham. A sense of the ridiculous returned and I giggled at my inability to control my shaking body. Graham and Peter cursed ineffectually but John began to moan and they stopped. The shivering became spasmodic as the breeze died and an uneasy silence returned. The others dropped into a half sleep while I stared at the indifferent stars. Their patterns appeared to change perceptibly and I was filled with a vast vision of the slowly rotating earth.

When I next woke the quality of light had changed and I realised that the dawn had begun. All sense of romance or beauty had gone in the miserable half light. The cold was intense, the world was dead.

Though the light grew and the opportunity had come to move again, there was reluctance to give up our stiff, huddled positions; there was a special agony in shifting cramped limbs and making them work again. But with great effort I sat upright and forced iron-hard boots on to my feet. My fingers lost all feeling as I exposed them to the air and struggled with frozen laces, willing them to work. Finally, I staggered to my feet and began stamping rhythmically. Slowly the others came to life and joined me, stamping, working arms back and forth. Grunts turned to words and at last I was moved to comment on the glorious flush of pink that graced the highest peaks.

After a mouthful of cold water, I persuaded Graham to rope up and secure me while I tried to hack a way into and across the crevasse. There was still no guarantee that we could get down.

Carefully I climbed over the rim of our bivouac hollow and began cutting steps down a curved sheet of ice which led into the crevasse. With one hand braced against the ice, I swung the axe with the other, livening to the task as muscles warmed. The slope steepened and I banged in a steel spike to secure the rope in case I slipped. Seven blows and scrapes of the axe for each step, two steps then move down and begin again. Two steps at a time, neck craning to see what opening or impasse lay at the bottom of the slope.

Graham called that only ten feet of rope remained. I moved a little further and saw, to my delight, that the ice sheet finished on a small buttress of rock in the middle of the crevasse. A narrow but solid bridge of ice rose from it to the far lip. I shouted with joy.

The others followed me down to the glacier and we moved on in a dangerous mood of optimism. All our problems seemed to be over. But Graham twice slid down the hard snow and suddenly I was aware that a careless state of mind was as menacing as any of the huge crevasses that lacerated the glacier. It looked like a great amphitheatre, the crevasses forming tiers, but there was no aisle from one to the other.

Soon our mood was sobered as we wandered along the edge of the next crevasse: it stretched unbroken to the far side of the glacier. Tightly I controlled a renewed feeling of desperation and plodded on grimly in the hope of sudden release.

The sun was higher now, easing the grip of frost. A warning rumble came from the seamed face above, then there was a brief silence before the crack and rattle of ricocheting stones as they hurtled down to the glacier. I watched fascinated as they spun over the ice, gouged into the snow and slid to rest below the crevasse. There lay the way out.

We climbed higher until we could see into the rotten-rock gully from which the debris had fallen. Below, tons of rubble had pulverised the ice and filled the crevasse. The crossing would be dangerous and our move would have to be timed for a pause in the stone fall; but if we waited long, the warming air would unfreeze the rock entirely and there would be constant bombardment.

Another shower of stones hummed past, then we followed it with a rush on to the glassy, pitted ice, slithering and sliding to safety. As fast as our legs would allow we scrambled over the pile of rocks at the bottom and ploughed into clean snow again, feeling in our bones that we had overcome the last obstacle. A few minutes later we moved into the sun and could see across the final undulations of the glacier to our undisturbed tracks of the day before. Feeling very tired, I stopped and peeled off my parka and sweaters, still partly frozen, and watched the seams of ice change to beads of glistening water.

An hour later we moved off the last snow and stopped to unrope. I looked up at the mountain that was unchanged and unmoved by our little adventure. My companions sat on rocks stowing equipment into their packs, preparing for the long trudge home down the valley. The day before we had tied together as four individuals teamed to climb a mountain, to follow a chosen sport. Now there was a difference that defied words: a fragile bond had been formed by a common experience of adversity; for a few hours each had been essential to another's comfort or well-being. Though the mountain was indifferent, it had been a proving ground, and I was now vastly more aware of myself and of those who had been with me.

The intangible emotions that filled us brought no special words, only new tones of expression, a sense of closeness as we shared the last remnants of food. The relationship would not last long; but there would be the memory of an experience that had shaped us all. That would be enough.

Fresh snow on tussock

Mount Hooker from the Haast River

Mount Tasman at sunset

Evening light on the Fritz Range, with gorge of the Franz Josef Glacier behind and the Almer Glacier beyond

*Overleaf* Last light on the summit of Mount Cook (foreground) and Mount Tasman

OTHER BOOKS BY PHILIP TEMPLE

*Nawok!*
(The N.Z. New Guinea Expedition, 1961)

*The Sea and the Snow*
(The South Indian Ocean Expedition to Heard Island, 1964-5)

*The World at their Feet*
(The story of New Zealand mountaineers in the great ranges of the world)

All the author's photographs were taken with Asahi Pentax Sla 35mm single lens reflex cameras with 35mm, 55mm, 105mm and 200mm lenses. Skylight filters were used for all colour work and extensive use was made of yellow (and orange) filters for black and white photography. Colour film used was Kodachrome II, with some Ektachrome and High Speed Ektachrome. Black and white film used was mostly Kodak Plus-X.

Dawn over Malte Brun Range